LEARN SPANISH

FOR BEGINNERS

A COMPLETE GUIDE OF HOW TO LEARN SPANISH FROM SCRATCH

WHITE BELT MASTERY

© **Copyright 2021 - All rights reserved.**

The contents of this book may not be reproduced, duplicated, or transmitted without direct written permission from the author.

Under no circumstances will any legal responsibility or blame be held against the publisher for any reparation, damages, or monetary loss due to the information herein, either directly or indirectly.

Legal Notice:

This book is copyright protected. This is only for personal use. You cannot amend, distribute, sell, use, quote, or paraphrase any part of the content within this book without the consent of the author.

Disclaimer Notice:

Please note the information contained within this document is for educational and entertainment purposes only. Every attempt has been made to provide accurate, up to date, and reliable complete information. No warranties of any kind are expressed or implied. Readers acknowledge that the author is not engaging in the rendering of legal, financial, medical, or professional advice. The content of this book has been derived from various sources. Please consult a licensed professional before attempting any techniques outlined in this book.

By reading this document, the reader agrees that under no circumstances is the author responsible for any losses, direct or indirect, which are incurred as a result of the use of the information contained within this document, including, but not limited to, —errors, omissions, or inaccuracies.

A few words before moving forward...

Spanish is now considered **the second most spoken language** in the world.

Due to a massive migration, culture impact, music and many other aspects, Spanish is now heard even in a tiny dance bar in Greece or Russia.

This can be translated as tons of people willing to start learning a new language and also willing to visit Spanish speaking countries which now-a-days are 21.

So **why learning Spanish?** Even though English keeps being the «international language» now on this multicultural world, Spanish is starting to get relevant and become interesting for people like artists, travelers, influencers and you who decided to buy this book and give the first step into this amazing romance language!

This book has the purpose of helping you through the basics of Spanish with step-by-step explanations, short dialogues, vocabularies and exercises, so, at the end of these pages, you will be able to introduce yourself, talk about events in the present or past tense, give opinions about specific situations, use adjectives, adverbs, pronouns, how to conjugate verbs and much more... All this will help you move from totally zero to a beginner-advanced level.

This book will become your guide during the first steps of this journey and will give you all the tools you need in order to start learning this beautiful language full of culture!

Glossary

Within the pages of this book you might encounter different words you might not be familiar with. To create an easier environment, here is a complete glossary with most of the complex words you will find in this book.

A

Adjective: an adjective is a word that will describe a person or thing. For example: red, blue, big, tall, short…

Adverb: an adverb is a word that will describe how the action is happening, it could be a location, a way, timing… For example: quickly, early, bad, well, fast…

Affix: is a word placed before or after a word to create a new different one, related to its root. For example: vice-president, antibacterial…

C

Clause: a clause is a main part of the sentence; a complete or partial idea can be obtained from a clause.

Complement: a complement is a part of the sentence that gives meaning to it.

D

Deictic: is a word related to the meaning of a verb that changes according to the speaker or listener

N

Noun: a noun is a word that have an identity by itself: For example: dog, house, man, chicken…

O

Object: in grammar, an object is a noun that is being affected by a verb's action

P

Pronoun: a pronoun is a word that can replace longer nouns or identities, for example: you, me, she, her, mine…

Prefix: a prefix is a word that is placed before a main structure. For example: sub-zero, antibacterial, independent…

S

Subject: is a synonym of noun, it's a word that has identity

Suffix: is a word placed at the end of a structure to add or modify its meaning. Presidential, sailor, maritime…

Sentence: a sentence is a consecutive structure composed of different small structures or parts that do not have explain ideas. For example: the dog is my friend.

T

Tense: in grammar a tense is a category that explains or make reference to the time where an action happens, happened, will happen…

Index

Introduction 1
   The main part of communication: the sentence 2
   The parts of the sentence: noun and complement 4
   The Variation in Spanish 12
   Spanish vs. English 13

Chapter 1: ¡Hola! Welcome to Spanish 16
   Part I – Greetings.. 17
   Part II – Introducing ourselves 21
   Part III – Genders... 26
   Part IV – Nationalities 35
   Part IV – Singular & Plural Form... 37

Chapter 2: Verbs in Present Tense (Indicative) 46
   Part I: Conjugation groups 47
   Part II: Sentences: Affirmative, Negative and Interrogative Form 56
   Part III: Verb "Gustar" 68
   Part IV: Copulative Verbs "Ser" and "Estar" 78
   Part VI: Deictic Verbs.. 105
   Part VI: Verbal Periphrasis 120

Chapter 3: Dates, Numbers and Time 125
   Part I: Numbers 126

Part II: Telling the time 141

Part II: The date... 144

Chapter 4: Possessives.. 147

Part I: Possessive adjectives.. 147

Part II: Genitive "'s" in Spanish 152

Chapter 5: Sentence Complements 154

Part I: Direct Complement or Direct Object 156

Part II: Indirect Complement or Indirect Object....................... 160

Part III: Circumstantial Complement 169

Chapter 6: Sentences from a syntactic point of view 173

Part I: Predicative sentences 174

Part II: Copulative or Attributive Sentences 176

Chapter 7: Adverbs.. 178

Part I: Adverbs (Definition and Classification).......................... 179

Part II: Variation 182

Chapter 8: Creativity of the Spanish language 184

Part I: Derivation... 185

Vocabulary.. 191

Introduction

With the content of this introduction, we do not intend to make you an expert in Spanish grammar. The notions to be presented are aimed at understanding and improving the quality of your productions, both orally and written in Spanish, in a conscious way. Although grammatical, syntactic and morphological aspects will be explained further on the first chapter and on, it is important to dwell more specifically before moving forward; so, from this part until the end, we will make emphasis on its more standard use. In other words, you will be able to learn what we can consider to be the basic grammar for the use of Spanish that this book offers you.

Content

- Sentence
- Phrase
- Main sentence
- Subordinate clause / sentence
- Noun
- Predicate
- The variety in Spanish
- Relevant differences between English and Spanish

The main part of communication: the sentence

> As a starting point, you should know that in Spanish, as in any language, you can express through phrases, sentences or a set of these. The sentence is a linguistic structure with a complete communicative sense organized around a verb.

In the Spanish, the structure of a simple sentence is exactly the same as in Spanish "noun + verb + complement" although the grammatical terminology can change (e.g. "*Clauses*") it's easy to find the sense in almost all of the cases or situations in Spanish.

Here's a detailed explanation about the types of sentences in Spanish:

The **main clause** or *"Oración Principal"* in Spanish, is the one that does not depend on another element (verb or noun) that it qualifies and determines. It is characterized by having a verb, probably a subject and perhaps some complements. For example: *La chica a la que conocí cuando estuve en España ha venido esta mañana porque quiere conocer a mis padres.* / **"The girl that I met when I was in Spain, has come this morning because (she) wants to meet my parents"**

Noun **(N)**	La chica a la que conocí cuando estuve en España
Verb **(V)**	ha venido
Circumstantial Complement **(CC)**	esta mañana porque quiere conocer a mis padres

The **subordinate clause** or *"Oración Subordinada"*, like the main one, is characterized by having a verb, probably a subject and perhaps some complements. But it is not independent, on the contrary, it forms part of another (main) clause in which it performs some of the typical functions of nouns, adjectives or adverbs. In the previous example we have 4 subordinate clauses:

1. *la que conocí <u>cuando estuve en España</u>.* It is an adverbial subordinate clause because, like the adverb, it qualifies, characterizes or defines a noun: The girl / **La chica...**

2. *cuando estuve en España.* It is a temporal adverbial subordinate clause, because it defines, like temporal adverbs to the verb, met: When I met / **Cuando conocí...**

3. *porque quiere conocer a mis padres.* It is a causal adverbial subordinate clause, because it defines the reason why happened what's indicated by the verb: has come: She has come because ... / **Ha venido porque...**

4. *conocer a mis padres.* Objective substantive subordinate clause, it is substantive because it is located where we would normally have a noun based on a direct object: **she wants to...**

With this short explanation we wanted to show you how sentences or clauses are structured in Spanish and some of the types in which they are classified. On the next paragraphs, you will find more details about the other parts of the basic grammar topics.

The parts of the sentence: noun and complement

When talking about the complement in Spanish, there's no big difference compared to English. Although, the noun has two different ways you can "observe it" in a sentence and it's an important characteristic in Spanish.

The Noun / El Sujeto

The syntax teaches us that the words have their particular functions, that allows us to know them as categories or classes of words.

The particular functions are the characteristics of a word class; the ones that only it can perform. Thus, only the noun can be the nucleus of the subject; only the modifying adjective of the subject.

The Spanish language offers many possibilities in its realization in speech (oral / written), hence the importance of knowing its possibilities, however synthetic the information may be. It is important to know that **words by their proprietary functions are classified into nine categories, all of which are treated with special care in this book. These are: noun, adjective, article, verb, adverb, preposition, conjunction and interjection.**

The following lines are dedicated to the noun. We will comment on its syntactic, morphological, semantic and usage aspects which are more appropriate and relevant for those who learn this foreign language.

To recognize the noun, we must ask ourselves who or what performs the action indicated in the verb or who / what we are characterizing.

It is important to note that it is normally the nouns that function as subjects, but there are other categories that can do so. For example:

- A pronoun: He speaks / "**Él** habla"
- A noun as adjective: The red ones are good / "**Las rojas** son buenas"
- An infinitive verb: Eating is good / "**Comer es bueno**"

Other details that allow us to recognize the subject:

- It agrees in number and person with the verb (e.g. *the children eat the soup*).
- The subject is not preceded by a preposition (except in the case of the preposition between, for example, between you and I we will).

Classification of the noun or subject:

- By absence or presence:
    - Express: Alicia spoke / "**Alicia habló**"
    - Tacitus (omitted): We speak / "**Hablamos**" (The omitted noun is "we").
- By the number of cores:
    - Simple (one core). The lion roared / "**El león rugió**"
    - Compound (two or more cores). The tiger and the lion roared / "**El tigre y el león rugieron**"

The omitted noun is a very common structure in Spanish, a long sentence can go along all of the conversation by just having a single noun, in fact, in a common conversation, a noun will be used only if the conversation is long as it has multiple nouns involved. Although, a Spanish speaker can understand who's doing the action just by the way the verb is conjugated.

The noun designates material and immaterial elements of reality. Apart from the privilege of being the nucleus of the subject or the noun phrase, the noun by itself names the objects, the people, the countries, etc. A noun, given the lexical richness of Spanish, can be replaced by another (synonym noun) or also by a pronoun.

The noun like the article has gender (feminine, masculine) and number (singular and plural). These characteristics must always coincide with those of the article, which almost always accompanies the noun.

In addition to nouns (common and proper nouns) there are other types of words that can adopt the function of a noun such as an infinitive verb (with or without an article), a noun adjective or an adverb (always preceded by an article).

Examples of the first case are:
> **Smoking** is bad / "**Fumar** es malo"
> **Arriving** early is a virtue / "**Llegar** temprano es una virtud"

When the noun is an adjective:
> **The electric one** is the future (the car or the electric car) / "**El eléctrico** es el futuro.

How nouns work in Spanish

There's an interesting fact in Spanish when talking about nouns/subjects. In general, the noun can be placed after the verb, just like in English. E.g. *José arrives at home* / "José llega a la casa".

But in some very specific cases, **a noun can be placed after the verb it (the noun) is conjugating.** E.g. *Arrives Joseph at home* / Llega José a la casa.

Here are other specific examples:

> **The car** doesn't work / "No funciona **el carro**" or "**El carro** no funciona"

> **(The) people** can understand themselves by talking / "**La gente** se entiende hablando" or "Hablando se entiende **la gente**"

> 💡 This "style" or possibility is related to the capacity or ability in Spanish to switch the parts of a sentence's order. Spanish speakers choose -in a common way- the specific situation in which the orders can be changed without sounding awkward or bizarre. Although, as a Spanish learner, maybe you might like to learn when you can apply this changes, but two things are important to understand: that these are not necessary and it's a common situation so from now on, you can realize that speaking like Yoda is sometimes natural in Spanish, and, with experience, you can put this in practice too!

Noun modifiers:

In general, in Spanish, the noun is modified by: a direct modifier, a complement, a comparative construction, an apposition or a proposition. These parts can be switched or placed in different parts of the sentences and their meanings remain the same. **In some situations, changing the position of a sentence's part might change the tone into a *"poetic"* or more formal style.** By practicing (reading this book, talking to Spanish speakers, watching tv, listening to music) you can note these situations and boost your improvement in Spanish.

Observe these examples to know a bit more about how nouns are modified.

Examples:

> The radiant day / "El día radiante". The noun *"day"* has a direct modifier (radiant).

These kinds of modifiers can be placed before the noun and the meaning remains the same. In Spanish, changing or *"playing"* with these positions are used to sometimes give a rhetorical style. For example: *The cold night* / "La noche fría" (which sounds more common) or "La fría noche" (which would sound more "poetical" in Spanish).

> There are ways you can understand this. One of those is by learning how adjectives are or can be placed in Spanish sentences. Forward on this book you will find this topic which will help you a lot in improving this skill.

The morphology of the noun

The noun can undergo modifications or morphological changes both in the base and in the termination, depending on the particular case. This is generally due to two grammatical accidents: gender and numbers.

> **Gender:** in Spanish there are feminine and masculine nouns, contrary to English which does not have them for almost all words. Check these points to understand this topic:
>
> **Masculine:**
> o **Because of its meaning:**
>   The male names (animals and people like *father, man, boy*)

The name of rivers, mountains, seas and cordilleras
Profession when a male noun performs it
The months, days and cardinal points
- **Because of its termination:**
Those who end with vowel, except for "a"
Some words from Greek origin ending with "a" (The poet, the poem, the artist)

Feminine:

- **Because of its meaning:**
The female names (animals and people like *mother, woman, girl*)
Professions when a female noun performs it
The letters of the alphaber
The arts and subjects (math, arts, science, painting, sculpturing, music) "dancing" is an exception
Words ending with vowel "a" with some minimal exceptions

- **Because of its termination:**
Those who end with vowel, except for "a"
Some words from Greek origin ending with "a" (The poet, the poem, the artist

There are some nouns that indicate people or animals and have two endings of their own (they have generic variation). For example:

    aunt/uncle *in Spanish* **"tío/tía"**

    boy/girl *in Spanish* **"niño/niña"**

There are nouns that do not vary in termination. They are classified into masculine or feminine, according to the adjective that can accompany them (they have a generic attraction) For example:

    the ancient ship *in Spanish* **"La nave antigua"**

    the pretty aircraft *in Spanish* **"El avión bonito"**

where feminine words have an adjective ending in "a" and masculine words have an adjective ending in "o".x

> **Numbers:** in Spanish, nouns can exist in singular and plural form. They will follow rules, similar to English language like adding the letter "s" to change the noun into its plural form. Some others commonly exist in plural form like *"googles"* and of course as in any other language, there are exceptions. This point will be further explained in the chapters below.

The Predicate

To recognize the predicate of a sentence, simply ask for the action that the subject is said to perform. For this, first of all, we must locate the nucleus of the predicate: the main verb.

In Spanish this part of the sentences can vary on its position but its easily understandable or recognizable.

Classification of the predicate in Spanish:

- Verbal: by the number of nuclei:
  - Simple (one core). <u>Walk</u> a lot. / **"Camina mucho"**
  - Compounds (two or more nuclei). He <u>walks and runs</u> a lot. / **"Camina y corre mucho"**
- For the syntactic class of verbs:
  - With copulative verb (requires mandatory predicate). The night is dark / **"La noche está oscura"**
  - With a non-copulative verb, if it has a predicative, it is not mandatory: Luis <u>reads quietly</u> / **"Luis lee tranquilo"**
- Non-verbal nominal: The nucleus is a noun or an adjective: My dad, <u>a great person</u>. / **"Mi papá, una gran persona"**
- Non-verbal adverbial: the nucleus is an adverb or an equivalent construction.

    - <u>There</u>, a mailbox. / **"Allí, un buzón"**

    - <u>In the center</u>, the table. / **"En el centro, una mesa"**

There are different types but there are no big differences when translating into Spanish, as you could observe. As an interesting fact, the predicate or complement can change their positions in the sentence and without affecting its sense or meaning.

The Variation in Spanish

> When the multiple territories were colonized by the Spaniards, they brought people from all over their kingdom, and they also brought African slaves, who were in their majority, taken to the Caribbean islands and the coasts of Latin America. This caused native people and African slaves to start learning the Spanish language - which was spoken with different accents/dialects – with no previous education, therefore, every small territory started adapting or creating vocabulary, varying personal pronouns, and developing slangs.

As a result, now millions of people are considered Spanish speakers and it's spoken in more than 20 countries. And every country has a slightly different accent, vocabulary and specially, slangs.

But the Spanish language is only "one" and no matter the country or the small town on top of a far icy mountain you're visiting, everyone will understand you. From every different country you visit or from every new Spanish-speaking friend you meet, you can learn a lot of interesting things, tons of funny idioms and many different accents!

The main differences in Spanish

Nowadays, there's an interesting discussion about what's the "variant" of Spanish that every country speaks. Some people say there's a Castillian Spanish which is spoken in Latin America and there are others that say there's a European Spanish, spoken in Spain.

Even though, there's a big, noticeable difference between the two main variants of Spanish, the one spoken in Latin America, and the one spoken in Spain.

In most of the territory of Spain, there's the use of the pronoun *"Vosotros"* which can be translated as the plural second-person *"you"* in English. But this pronoun is not used in any of the Latin American countries nor in the Caribbean territory. In these territories and some parts of Spain, this pronoun is replaced by *"Ustedes"*.

Another relevant difference is the sound of letter "c" and "z" is similar to the English "th" like *"thumb"*. This sound is a common characteristic of European Spanish and it can't be heard commonly in the rest of the Spanish speaking countries. On the contrary, both sounds will always be heard as the sibilant "s" in English when it's in words like *"serpent"* or *"house"*.

Then we have very "European" words like *"Enhorabuena"* which means "Congratulations" or a common slang *"Tío"* which means "buddy/pal". These two words are not common any other region.

To conclude this idea, for every country you visit, you will most likely learn how to say different things; like food, clothes, idioms and slangs. But remember, **the Spanish you will learn with this book, will be understood** in no matter the place you're visiting or the friend you are talking with.

Spanish vs. English

As a last point, and before moving to the interesting world of learning Spanish, it is important to remember that when you are speaking a different language, you have to *think* in that language, your brain needs to adapt to the structure of this new target in order to make the process easier and of course, to avoid common mistakes and false cognates.

Here's a list of the biggest differences in Spanish which would give you an idea and help your learning process through this book:

- **The nouns:** in English, they have no gender while in Spanish there are three and it also has a system of articles to answer questions about gender. This is one of the reasons why we say that English grammar is easier.

- **Adjectives:** they go before the noun in English, in Spanish they are generally postponed, although an adjective before the noun could be equally intelligible.

- **The negation:** In English the negation is simple, it is only denied once, in Spanish, the normal is to deny twice.

- **The Saxon genitive**: which typical of English and not Spanish. With the genitive any noun becomes a possessive. In Spanish, these links are resolved with the preposition <de>: Carlos's car. / "**El carro de Carlos**"

- **The explicit subject**: it is essential in English while in Spanish we can and usually omit it, once it is named or referred to in the speech.

- **The order of the sentence components:** this practically is unchanged in English. Conjugations are not necessary in the verbs with respect to the genres or the declensions. But the meaning of a sentence breaks ambiguities just by maintaining the order of its elements. In Spanish there is more flexibility because the meaning of the sentence is not altered much if the position of its elements is changed.

- **Capital letters and punctuation marks:** in English, they are used slightly differently than they are in Spanish. The days of the week, months of the year, and languages are written in English with an initial capital letter, but this doesn't happen in

Spanish because they are considered common names. Exclamation and question marks are used only when closing sentences, in Spanish, at the beginning and end of sentences. Exclamation marks: "¡!" and Interrogative marks "¿?".

Of course, as you get to know more of the Spanish language, you will find much more differences, but from the outset it is very positive that you can understand those listed above. They will help you a lot in this journey that's just barely beginning!

Chapter 1:

¡Hola! Welcome to Spanish

During this chapter you'll start learning how to begin a conversation in Spanish. An important part to take into consideration is that, compared to English, Spanish has pronouns for formal and informal situation depending on who are you talking with, is it a friend? Is it someone older? Is it someone you just meet but is young? Now, take a deep look at how people say "hi" in this amazing language.

Content

- Say "hi" (Formal and Informal way)
- Say "good-bye" (Formal and Informal way)
- Thank someone in Spanish
- Referring to a specific moment of the day
- Introduce yourself (two forms)
- Personal Pronouns
- Introducing reflexive verbs & reflexive pronouns
- The genders in nouns, articles and adjectives
- Nationalities
- Singular and plural forms

Part I – Greetings

> Spanish people are very kind and like to express emotions through words. You can easily become friend with someone in a Spanish culture but it doesn't mean there's no formal situation in which you have to sound polite. **Check the ways you can start a conversation!**

Informal way to say "hi":

- Hello / **"Hola"**
- How are you? / **"¿Cómo estás (tú)?"** (Conjugated with the informal pronoun "Tú")
- How are you doing? / **"¿Cómo vas (tú)?"**
- What's up? / **"¿Qué más?"**
- Everything's good? / **"¿Todo bien?"**
- I'm fine and you? / **"(Yo) estoy bien, ¿y tú?"**

Informal way to say "good-bye":

- Good-bye; bye / **"Chao"** : **"Adiós"**
- Take care / **"Cuídate"**

In most of the Latin-American countries "adiós" would be used only when you are saying good-bye to someone you won't see again.

Formal way to say "hi"

- Hello / **"Saludos"**

- How are you? / **"¿Cómo está (usted)?"** (Conjugated with the formal pronoun "Usted")
- How is it going? / **"¿Qué tal?"** (A bit more formal situation)
- Good and you? / **"Bien, ¿y usted?"** (See the "Usted" pronoun is used instead of "Tú")

Informal way to say "good-bye":

- See you soon / **"Hasta luego"**
- See you / **"Nos vemos"**

💡 In Spanish, there's a **formal pronoun "Usted"** only when referring to the second person "you" and it's used to sound polite. When you are in a meeting, talking to someone older you don't know or even your parents, you might have to use this instead of **informal "Tú"**.

Referring to a specific moment of the day

- Good day / **"Buen día"** – **"Buenos días"** (the difference in Spanish is singular or plural form which might change according to the country but is not relevant)
- Good afternoon / **"Buenas tardes"** (In Spanish there's no evening and afternoon it's used from 12pm to 6pm)
- Good night / **"Buenas noches"** (it's used from 7pm and on and it doesn't change if it's as a "greeting" or as a "good-bye
- See you soon / **"Hasta pronto"**
- See you tomorrow / **"Hasta mañana"**
- See you later / **"Te veo luego"**

➢ Have a nice day / **"Que tengas un buen día"**

> As you can see, there's no difference between formal and informal when talking about a specific moment of the day, which means this can only vary according to each individual and the word he/she wants to use in a determined situation.

Exercise 1: Read the following conversation and choose if it's formal or informal

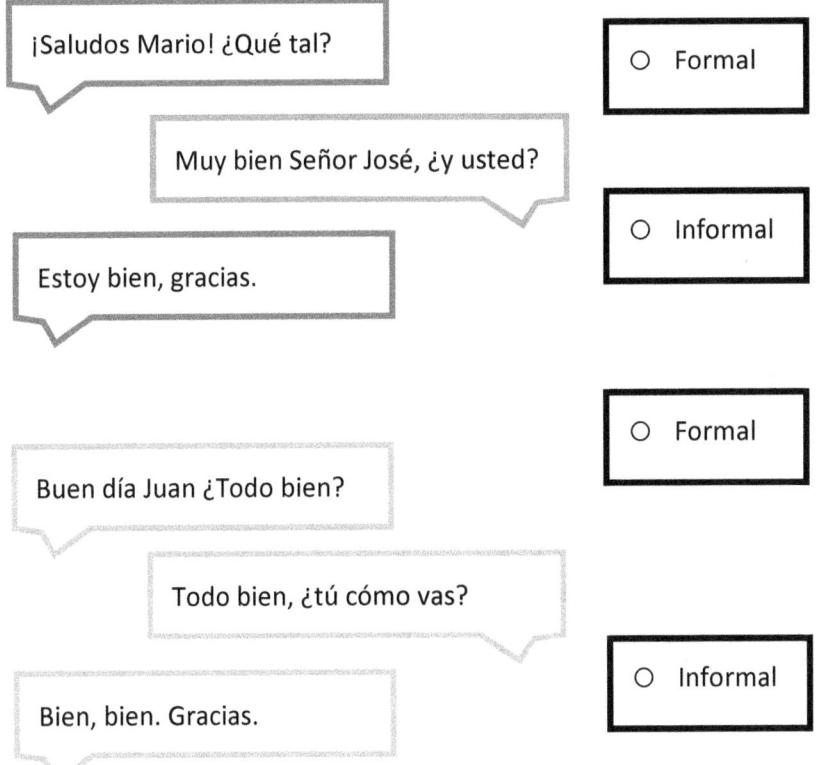

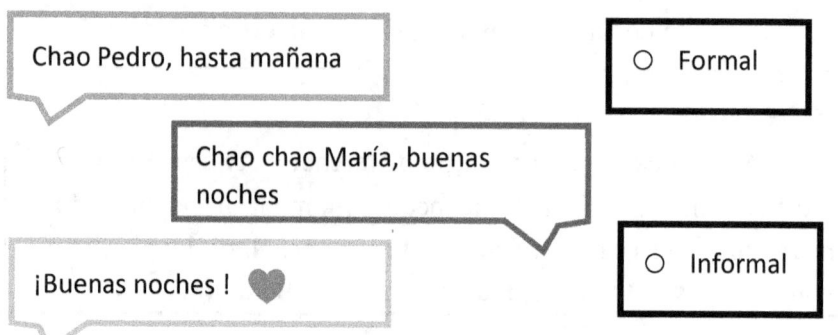

Exercise 2.1: Translate the following sentences into Spanish. Pay attention to the context!

a. Hi my friend! How are you?

b. Good morning Mr. Samuel, how are you?

c. What's up Daniel? How are you doing?

d. Good bye my friend. See you tomorrow

e. Good morning Ana, how is it going?

Exercise 2.2: Translate the following sentences into English.

a. Hola buen día ¿qué tal?

b. Hasta mañana Señor Carlos

c. Adiós amigo, nos vemos pronto
_____

d. Buenas noches Alejandro, ¿Cómo estás?
_____

e. Buenos días Ana, ¿Todo bien?
_____

Part II – Introducing ourselves

> In Spanish, there are multiple ways you can introduce yourself by using different verbs. On this part, you'll learn the common forms you can conjugate these verbs to talk about your identity. But first, let's take a look at the personal pronouns in Spanish.

Personal Pronouns:

Yo	I	
Tú	You	
Él / Ella	He / She	
Nosotros / Nosotras	We (Masculine/Feminine)	
Usted	You (Polite)	
Ustedes	You (plural) i.e. you guys	It's irrelevant if it's a group of people you know or you don't.
Ellos / Ellas	They (Masculine/Feminine)	

> 💡 There are a couple of differences here compared to English. In Spanish, the third-person, singular neuter pronoun **"It"** doesn't exist or at least not in the same way, so for a "neuter noun" you have to use either **"él"** or **"ella"**.
>
> On the other hand, it's very important to use the proper gender when using the plurals **"we"** and **"they"** in Spanish. Also, to complete the idea, **what happens when you have a group of women and men?** When that's the case, you will **always use the masculine form**.

When introducing yourself in Spanish, you have two forms, **using a Reflexive Verb** or by literally saying **"My name is…."** like "Mi nombre es".

- **A reflexive verb** is a verb composed by its infinitive form + a <u>reflexive pronoun</u>.

- When conjugating a reflexive verb, the reflexive pronoun goes first and then the verb, and they can't be mixed, so the conjugation has to match always (yo + me + llamo…tú te llamas…)

- Reflexive verbs, most of the time, **don't work the same way** as in English, so, literal translation won't be useful as a method for better understanding.

- **As a final point,** you better think in your mind as if you are saying "I call myself…" because that's a closer translation and it's actually how Spanish speakers introduce themselves.

Let's start with the first reflexive verb:

Reflexive Verb "Llamarse"

Personal Pronoun	Reflexive Pronoun	**Verb**
Yo	me	llamo
Tú	te	llamas
Él / Ella	se	llama
Nosotros / Nosotras	nos	llamamos
Usted	se	llama
Ustedes	se	llaman
Ellos / Ellas	se	llaman

Examples:

Read these short conversations to see how you can introduce yourself using both ways.

Conversation 1:

Hola ¿Cómo te llamas?

Hi, what's your name?

Me llamo Carlos, ¿y tú?

My name is Carlos, and you?

Me llamo María. Un placer.

My name is Maria. It's a pleasure

Conversation 2:

Mi nombre es Juan ¿y el tuyo?

My name is Juan and yours?

Mi nombre es Andrea. Encantada

My name is Andrea. It's a pleasure

Conversation 3:

¿Tienes hijos?

Do you have children?

Sí, tengo dos.

Yes, I have two.

¿Cómo se llaman?

What's their name?

Se llaman Juan y Paola.

They're called Juan and Paola.

⚠️ Attention! **Which one would you use** in real life? The difference between "Mi nombre es…" and "Me llamo…" is the "normality". Most of the time, people will use the conjugation of the reflexive verb "Me llamo" and in some few, minimal situations you will read or hear "Mi nombre es…".

Exercise 1: Complete the following sentences using either the reflexive pronoun or the conjugated for of the verb "llamarse" according to each sentence.

    a. Hola ___ llamo Juan

    b. ¿Qué tal? ¿Cómo te _____?

    c. Ellos ___ llaman Pedro y Pablo

    d. ¿Cómo ___ llaman _____?

    e. ¿Ella cómo ___ llama?

    f. Tú cómo ___ llamas?

Exercise 2: Read the following sentences and translate them into Spanish. Use always the reflexive verb "llamarse".

    a. Good morning, what's your name?
    _____

    b. Hello, my name is Alejandro.
    _____

    c. What's up? My name is Ana.
    _____

    d. Their names are María and José
    _____

    e. His name is Juan, her name is Juana.
    _____

Part III – Genders

> An important characteristic of Spanish is Gender, which are three: masculine, feminine and neutral which most of the time will be the masculine form of the word (nouns, articles…)
>
> Let's check the content starting from the rules about how to identify the gender and how to create/change words.

How to identify a masculine/female word:

The basic grammar rule consists in determining the gender by adding one of this two letters: **"o" or "a"** at the end of the word (noun, pronoun, article…) so in this language you can find similar words that can have the same letters but by changing the last one, it can be masculine or feminine. So, as you can see, adding or taking out letters in Spanish is a very common aspect. This is how this romance language works and it will happen always! In lexicology this is called "Lexical Family".

For example:

- **Gato** means "cat" but it's also explaining that it's a male cat.
- **Gata** means "cat" but it's also explaining that it's a female cat.

So you basically have the same three first letter "G-a-t" but by adding "o" or "a" you can switch between male or female gender. Let's see another example:

- **Niño** it's a boy
- **Niña** it's a girl

Here you have the same situation. "N-i-ñ" and adding "o" or "a" changes the word into boy or girl; "Niñ**o**" or "Niñ**a**".

From this easy rule you can identify, from now on, most of the genders for every noun in Spanish, it won't work for all of the Spanish vocabulary because, as in everything, there are exceptions. Here are some of them:

- ➢ **"Agua":** It means "water", and it seems female because of its last letter "a" but it's actually masculine in its singular form.
- ➢ **"Mano":** It means "hand", and it seems male because of its last letter "o" but it's actually feminine.

To complete this idea, then we have those who are called "neutrals" and they are the same for both masculine and feminine situation. Here some examples:

- ➢ **"Presidente":** It means "president", and it won't change no matter if it's a woman or a man.
- ➢ **"Dentista":** it means "dentist", and it's the same situation as the example above. It will keep the same structure whether it's a man or a woman.
- ➢ **"Músico":** This is Spanish for "Musician" and it won't change if it's a male or female musician.

Good news is that these are exceptions and just a handful of words in Spanish act like this, for the rest of the words, keep the rule "a" for feminine and "o" for masculine or neuter.

The Articles:

a. **Definite article "The":** Genders work in a lot of situations in Spanish. When talking about articles, these have to match with the gender of the noun, and in order to do this, you have to use the right translation for every situation. These are the 2 translations for the article "the" in its singular form:

- ➢ **"El"**: This is the male form of the article. It has to be used if the noun is masculine, for example:
    - The (male) dog / **"El perro"**
    - The (male) cat / **"El gato"**
    - The president (a man) / **"El presidente"**
    - The (male) student / **"El estudiante"**
    - The friend (a man, a boy….) / **"El amigo"**
    - The water / **"El agua"** as explained before, it's a "male" word

- ➢ **"La"**: This is the female form of the article. It has to be used if the noun is feminine, for example:
    - The house / **"La casa"**
    - The (female) cat / **"La gata"**
    - The (female) student / **"La estudiante"**
    - The friend (a woman, a girl…) / **"La amiga"**
    - The hand / **"La mano"** as explained before, it's a "female" word

As shown in these examples, you find words that you can/have to change according to who you are referring to like "el perro/la perra" or "el amigo/la amiga". Or words that, due to its definition, can't be changed such as "el agua", "la mano", "la casa" …

These nouns will always have the same "gender" so they can't have a different structure. Which means in Spanish, a house will be always a "feminine word" no matter how "masculine" you try to decorate it.

b. **Indefinite articles "a/an":** About these two words, in Spanish they work differently, first, they follow genders and second, they not necessarily have to change if the word starts with vowel or consonant. Let's give them a look in Spanish.

- ➢ **"Un":** This is the male form for the indefinite article. For example:
    - o A boy / **"Un niño"**
    - o A plane / **"Un avión"**
    - o A (male) dog / **"Un perro"**
    - o A seat / **"Un asiento"**
- ➢ **"Una":** This the female word for the indefinite article. For example:
    - o A girl / **"Una niña"**
    - o An adventure / **"Una aventura"**
    - o A house / **"Una casa"**
    - o A (female) friend / **"Una amiga"**

With these examples you can observe that it doesn't depend on the vowel or consonant, on the contrary, it depends on the gender.

Although, as you might guess, about indefinite articles, there are exceptions too. The nouns follow all the same grammar rule, and because of this, if you are using a definite or indefinite article, the exceptions will be always the same. Here are some you already know and some new:

- ➢ **"Agua":** which in case of saying "a water", it has to be "un agua", with the masculine article.
- ➢ **"Hacha":** it means "axe", and in case of saying "an axe", it has to be "un hacha".

There's a deep, grammar reason for this behavior. The explanation it's because, those words have stressed vowel at the beginning, and to avoid cacophony, Spanish uses the male form of the articles and by doing so, it sounds better.

For example:

- **A**gua has a stressed vowel at the beginning, so "a water/the water" becomes "un **a**gua/ el **a**gua".
- **Ha**cha has its stressed vowel at the beginning to and "an axe/the axe" becomes "un **ha**cha/ el **ha**cha".

Now you can have the complete idea about these exceptions that actually follow rules but different ones. Even though, trying to understand this is, at the same time, interesting and different, there are few words that follow this behavior, it's all about learning one by one and expanding your vocabulary!

Exercise 1: Complete the following nouns using the right definite article "el/la" according to their genders. (None of them behave as exceptions)

a. ____ perro
b. ____ casa
c. ____ amigo
d. ____ gato
e. ____ idea

Exercise 2: Complete the following nouns using the right indefinite article "un/una" according to their genders. (None of them behave as exceptions)

    a. ____ casa
    b. ____ amiga
    c. ____ amigo
    d. ____ artículo
    e. ____ niña

Adjectives

Adjectives also respond to the noun's gender. It has to change if it's a male or female situation, which means, words like "tall" will have a different translation for a male or a female noun.

Most of the time, they will follow the rule we've learned before: "a" is for female nouns and "o" is for male nouns.

Let's take a look at this idea:

- "Tall" in Spanish is: **"Alto/Alta"**
- "Short" or "Small" in Spanish is: **"Pequeño/Pequeña"**
- "Fat" in Spanish is: **"Gordo/Gorda"**
- "Pretty" in Spanish is: **"Bonito/Bonita"**

Another critical point is about the position of the adjective in a sentence. In English it goes before the noun as in "the **tall** boy" or "the **pretty** house". On the contrary, in Spanish they are commonly placed after the noun.

Thereby, a translation for "the tall boy" would be "el niño **alto**" or a different example like "the pretty house", in Spanish would be "la casa **bonita**".

And even if they are separated by "and" in an example like "*a small and fat dog*", both adjectives will be placed after the pronoun. Translation: "un perro **pequeño y gordo**".

See how it perfectly matches every component of the sentence according to the nouns' gender.

A common mistake would be to mistranslate one of the parts of the sentence, could be either the article, the noun or the adjective. For example: "el perra bonita" or "la casa pequeño". Instead of "la perra bonita" or "la casa pequeña".

So pay attention to every detail and take your time at the beginning to think and then realize what the right word you have to use is.

Are there any exceptions with adjectives? Yes, there are! And here's a small list of them:

- "Big" / **"Grande"**
- "Green" / **"Verde"**
- "Caliente" / **"Caliente"**
- "Increíble" / **"Increíble"**

For these words it doesn't matter the gender. So, you can say "a green house" or "a green car" with the same translation: "una casa **verde**" or "un auto **verde**".

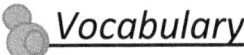
Vocabulary

Within this vocabulary you will find practical words for daily life which will come handy when speaking Spanish, they are divided into 3 categories. Some of them will have two translation (masculine/feminine) and some others, only one. Which means they can be neutrals and only have one form.

Colors	_Size_	_Appearance_
"Red" / **"Rojo(a) "**	"Small" / **"Pequeño(a)**	"Pretty" / **"Bonito(a)"**
"Blue" / **"Azul"**	"Big" / **"Grande"**	"Ugly" / **"Feo(a)"**
"Yellow"/ **"Amarrillo(a)"**	"Tall" / **"Alto(a)"**	"Beautiful / **"Hermoso(a)"**
"White" / **"Blanco(a)"**	"Fat" / **"Gordo(a)"**	"Handsome" / **"Guapo(a)"**
"Black" / **"Negro(a)**	"Skinny" / **"Flaco(a)"**	

Exercise 3: Translate the following sentences into Spanish

a. A white dog and a red house

_____

b. The beautiful (female)cat

_____

c. A tall and white boy

_____

d. The pretty girl

_____

e. A blue and beautiful house

_____

How adjectives can be placed in Spanish

To complete this point, remember in the Spanish, adjectives can switch their positions in the sentence. This is not the result of people speaking the way they want to, but the structured criteria which evolved with hundreds of years and now it's summarized in books, like this one.

By learning these standards, you can now have a better understanding of Spanish structure when talking about switching the position of an adjective related to the nucleus.

Standards:

- **Logical:** If the adjective is specific, it is placed after the nucleus.
    E.g. blue car / "Auto **azul**"
    If the adjective is explanatory it is placed before the nucleus.
    E.g. bad friends / "**Malos** amigos"

- **Psychological:** The adjective will go before the nucleus if it is subjective.
    E.g. good game / "**Buen** juego"

- **Rhythmic:** If the adjective is longer than the nucleus, it is written after it.
    E.g. scary boy / "Chico **asustadizo**"
    E.g. the untamable horse / "El caballo **indomable**"

- **Distribution:** If the adjective has little informative content, it is written before the nucleus.
    E.g. good shot / "Buen **tiro**"
    If the adjective has a higher degree of information, it is postponed.

E.g. solar panel / "Panel **solar**" and not "**solar** panel"

- **Significative:** The meaning changes if the adjective changes its position.
  E.g. In Spanish *"poor man"* have two different translations and they do not mean the same thing. In this case, that sentence can be translated as:
  "**Pobre** hombre" and "hombre **pobre**"
  In which the first one is related to a emotive condition more than economical, and the second translation is highly related to "money".

 Perfect practice makes perfect results!

Part IV – Nationalities

Nationalities are adjectives too because they identify someone or something. In this part, this book will show you how to use the most common nationalities in the world, qnd because they are adjectives, they need to match gender and quantity.

Most common nationalities:

America	Translation	Europe	Translation
American	**Americano(a)**	European	**Europeo(a)**
Latin-American	**Latinoamericano(a)**	Portuguese	**Portugués(a)**
Mexican	**Mexicano(a)**	Spaniard	**Español(a)**
Cuban	**Cubano(a)**	French	**Francés(a)**

Puerto Rican	**Puertorriqueño(a)**	Italian	**Italiano(a)**
Cuban	**Cubano(a)**	British	**Inglés(a)/Británico(a)**
Venezuelan	**Venezolano(a)**	German	**Alemán(a)**
Colombian	**Colombiano(a)**	Norwegian	**Noruego(a)**
Brazilian	**Brasileño(a)**	Irish	**Irlandés(a)**
Peruvian	**Peruano(a)**	Dutch	**Holandés(a)**
Bolivian	**Boliviano(a)**	Greek	**Griego(a)**
Argentinian	**Argentino(a)**	Dane	**Danés(a)**
Chilian	**Chileno(a)**	New zealander	**Neozelandés(a)**

Africa and Middle East	*Translation*	*Asia and Australia*	*Translation*
African	**Africano(a)**	Asian	**Asiático(a)**
Libyan	**Libanés(a)**	Chinese	**Chino(a)**
Congolese	**Congoles(a)**	Japanese	**Japonés(a)**
Nigerian	**Nigeriano(a)**	Korean	**Coreano(a)**
Senegalese	**Senegales(a)**	Russian	**Ruso(a)**
Angolese	**Angoles(a)**	Indian	**Hindú**
Arabian	**Árabe**	Filipino	**Filipino(a)**
Syrian	**Sirio(a)**	Australian	**Australiano(a)**
Egyptian	**Egipcio(a)**	Vietnamese	**Vietnamita**
Israelian	**Israelí**	Polynesian	**Polinesio(a)**
Turkish	**Turco(a)**	Taiwanese	**Taiwanés(a)**
Iranian	**Iraní**		

As you can observe, they vary according to the continent, but they are easy to learn, specially the Spanish-speaking countries, most of them use the suffixes *"-ano/ana"*. European countries vary but practice is always the key to learn!

Part IV – Singular & Plural Form

> In Spanish, all the parts of the sentence have to match, the articles need to be related to the nouns, and the verb will be conjugated according to it. If there's an adjective, the structure changes according to gender and quantity too.
>
> As in English, in a lot of situations, the single letter "s" will be used to change a word into its plural form.

To change a word into its plural form, a couple of rules needs to be followed:

- **If the word ends with vowel:** when a word can be changed into its plural form and it ends with a vowel, you have to add the letter "s". Here are some examples:

    Examples:
    Casa *becomes* Casas
    Perro *becomes* Perros
    Niño *becomes* Niños
    Mano *becomes* Manos

- **If the Word ends with consonant:** if a word ends with consonant (**except for "z"** as it has a different rule), you have to add "-es". Check these examples:

    Examples:
    Amor *becomes* Amores
    Canción *becomes* Canciones
    Azul *becomes* Azules

> **If the word ends with consonant "z":** in this case, the "z" in the word is replaced by "-ces".

   Examples:
   "Pencil" / Lápiz *becomes* lapi**ces**

> **If the word ends with "i":** even though, a word ending with this vowel is less common in Spanish, it has its own rule. In this case you have to add "-es" without replacing the letter "i".

   Examples:
   "Manatee" / Manatí *becomes* manat**íes**

It is important to remember that in Spanish, when a group of people/things is composed of male and female members, the male form (in singular or plural) will be always used.

As an interesting fact: due to the new era of equal rights, Spanish speakers can use both forms in a sentence, as a way to sound more inclusivist. For example:

- Niños y niñas
- Trabajadores y Trabajadoras
- Americanos y Americanas

Even though it's not mandatory, it's a popular practice nowadays.

To complete this idea, now when using adjectives, articles, nouns or learning new words like determinants, possessives… Always pay attention to their forms.

Let's continue with **the definite article "the" in its plural forms**.

The definite article "el/la" (Plural forms)

Singular Form		Plural form	
Masculine	Feminine	Masculine	Feminine
el	la	los	Las

As seen on the board, basically *"the"* in Spanish has four translations, singular (masculine and feminine) and plural (masculine and feminine), which means, when a noun is plural, the article must match the quantity and its gender. Here some examples:

- The boys / **"Los niños"**
- The houses / **"Las casas"**
- The hands / **"Las manos"**
- The (male) cats / **"Los gatos"**
- The (female) cats / **"Las gatas"**

Now, adjectives in English will also remain in singular form when is preceding a noun or at the end of a sentence. But in Spanish, if the noun is plural, the adjective has to be used in its plural form too, just the same way as with the definite articles. For example:

"The big house" / "La casa grande"	"The tall boy" / "El niño alto"
"The big houses" / "La**s** casa**s** grande**s**"	"The tall boys" / "Los niños altos"

"The blue car" / "El auto azul"	"The pretty cat" / "La gata bonita"
The blue cars" / "Los autos azules	"The pretty cats" / "Las gatas bonitas"

> 💡 This is a constant behavior that will happen in further in most of the new content you will learn in this book.

Exercise 1: Translate the following sentences into Spanish

a. *The big boys*
___

b. *The red houses*
___

c. *The small car*
___

d. *The pretty girl*
___

e. *The yellow (male) cats*
___

Let's continue with **the indefinite articles "a/an" in their plural forms**.

The indefinite article (Plural forms)

Singular Form		Plural form	
Masculine	Feminine	Masculine	Feminine
un	una	Unos	unas

The indefinite articles in Spanish have also plural forms. They can be translated as *"some"* and, as most of the words in Spanish, they have to match with the nouns' gender they are undefining.

Check these conversations to learn a bit more about how these articles work:

Conversation 1: At the bar

Context: Juan goes to the bar and ask for a drink.

> Hola quiero unas cervezas

> How much do the two cost?

> Hola, bueno tenemos unas baratas y unas más caras

> Hey, well we got some cheap ones and a few more expensive ones

> ¿Cuánto cuestan las dos?

> How much do the two cost?

> White 10 and Black 12

> Las blancas 10 y las negras 12

> Entonces quiero 4 blancas porfa.

> Then I want four white please.

Conversation 2: At school

Context: Andrés asks to the classroom if someone has seen his crayons. Carlos answers back.

> ¿Han visto unos crayones rojos por aquí?

> *Have you seen any red crayons around here?*

> *I saw some, they're on the teacher's desk, why?*

> Yo vi unos, están en el escritorio de la maestra ¿Por qué?

> *Thank you, Carlos, they're mine.*

> Gracias Carlos, es que son míos.

Conversation 3: At home

Context: Andrea talks to her boyfriend at home, she is going to go to the supermarket.

> *Alejandro, I'm going to the market to buy some stuff. You want something?*

> Alejandro voy al mercado a comprar unas cosas. ¿Quieres algo?

> *Yes, ¡some chocolate cookies please!*

> Sí, ¡unas galletas de chocolates porfa!

> *Give. I'll be back in a little while!*

> Dale. ¡Vuelvo en un rato!

Conversation 4: At home 2

Context: Andrea gets back from the supermarket.

This article can be used with the same frequency as in English.

The difference is that in Spanish will only be used when there's more than one thing you can't directly count or define "some friends" "some ideas" "some houses" "some objects" … and it's not strictly necessary in situations like "do you want some water?"

In fact, that sentence can be translated "do you want water?" as "¿Quieres agua?" without adding the "some".

Also, there's no need to answer or change this article into a different word depending on the sentence like the alternance between "some" and "any", i.e. "do you want **some** water? "I don't want **any** water".

Further in this book, you will learn about indefinite pronouns such as "something", "anything", "nothing" which have unique translations in Spanish and they are used in specific situations different from the plural indefinite article "some".

Chapter 2:

Verbs in Present Tense (Indicative)

On this chapter we'll explore how the verbs work in Spanish (in present tense). Most of the lexical structure stands on the same principles: words that are divided into simple forms (lexemes) and then they are mixed with other particles which together with lexemes, form a different word. These other particles are called morphemes. This "mixing" structure work for verbs too. You will see that when conjugating verbs, they keep the same "base" and will change the last letters.

Also is important -now that you're giving the first steps into this language, to have in mind that Spanish is divided into two big moods: indicative and subjunctive. All of the tenses you will learn in this book belongs to the indicative mood, which means that they are actions that are true, false, real and/or certain.

Content

- ➢ Conjugation groups (First, Second and Third group)
- ➢ Sentences: Affirmative/Negative form
- ➢ Sentences: Interrogative form

- Interrogative particles
- "Gustar"
- Copulative verbs "ser" & "estar"
- Prepositions (in/on/at) in Spanish
- Reflexive verbs
- Deictic verbs "ir/venir" & "llevar/traer"
- Verbal Periphrasis

Part I: Conjugation groups

> In Spanish there are three moods: indicative, imperative and subjunctive and each one has a unique way of conjugation. **The indicative mood** is the one we'll start learning on this book, from present tense up to simple past tense. Even though each mood and therefore each tense has a unique conjugation, they will be always divided into 3 groups (first, second and third)

First Group "-ar"

In this group, we find the majority of the verbs in Spanish, they are all regular verbs, which means they all follow the same rule, except for a few others which require a small change. Here's how you can conjugate them. Remember this is a rule, and all of the verbs in this group will keep the same behavior. Another interesting point about these verbs is that, when new situations require the implementation/creation of new words to describe actions related to technology for example, Spanish language will place them here because they are the easiest to conjugate. For example: To tweet, to post, to chat…

➤ **Conjugation rules for first group:** on this scheme you'll be to see how the first group of verbs is conjugated. Here are 3 common verbs:

Personal Pronoun	Hablar *(to speak/to talk)*	Caminar *(to walk)*	Escuchar *(to listen)*
Yo	hablo	camino	escucho
Tú	hablas	caminas	escuchas
Él / Ella	habla	camina	escucha
Nosotros / Nosotras	hablamos	caminamos	escuchamos
Usted	habla	camina	escucha
Ustedes	hablan	caminan	escuchan
Ellos / Ellas	hablan	caminan	escuchan

💡 You can notice that they are different actions but they all belong to the same first group.

You can also notice that conjugation for "él/ella" and "usted" is exactly the same.

Same situation with "Ustedes" and "Ellos/ellas". They have the same rule.

Althought, they are not placed in the same line because they make reference to a different pronoun and it avoids creating misinterpretation.

So, from now on, no matter what verb you learn in the future, **if it ends in "-er"** it will be easy to conjugate as **it will follow these same rules ALWAYS**.

Exercise 1: Complete the following sentences by using the right conjugation for each pronoun.

a. Yo _____ (cantar) una canción. / *I sing a song.*

b. Tú _____ (llamar) a un amigo. / *You call a friend.*

c. Nosotros _____ (caminar) en el parque. / *We walk at the park.*

d. Ustedes _____ (hablar) por teléfono. / *You (plural) talk by phone.*

e. El perro _____ (ladrar) mucho. / *The dog barks a lot.*

f. La niña _____ (escuchar) música. / *La niña escucha música.*

➢ **Verbs with small changes:** As explained before, even though they have the same rule, there are some few verbs that have an additional modification when conjugated. Here's a small list of them:

Personal Pronoun	**Jugar** *(to play)*	**Almorzar** *(to have lunch)*	**Contar** (to count/to tell)
Yo	j**ue**go	al**muer**zo	**cuen**to
Tú	j**ue**gas	al**muer**zas	**cuen**tas
Él / Ella	j**ue**ga	al**muer**za	**cuen**ta

Nosotros / Nosotras	jugamos	almorzamos	contamos
Usted	j**ue**ga	al**muer**za	**cuen**ta
Ustedes	j**ue**gan	al**muer**zan	**cuen**tan
Ellos / Ellas	j**ue**gan	al**muer**zan	**cuen**tan

With these examples there are some few things to check:

- The vowel between the two consonants changes into two vowels.

    Jugar *becomes* j**ue**g- **contar** *becomes* c**ue**nt-

- This doesn't happen with every verb; these are just exceptions.
- The conjugation for "nosotros/nosotras" loses this change and will keep the same base from the verb. This happens always.

    Jugar *remains* jugamos **contar** *remains* contamos

Second Group "-er"

In this group, we find very common verbs, but these are also irregular verbs.

Irregular verbs will slightly change their bases, but the affixes (the letters added to the word), will remain the same within the second group verb rules.

Regular verbs will have the same behavior but they exist in less quantity in this group so, compared to the first group, here you do need to identify each verb and check if it's regular or irregular.

> **Conjugation rules for second group (regular verbs):** on this scheme you'll be to see how the second group of verbs is conjugated. Here are 3 regular verbs:

Personal Pronoun	<u>Comer</u> *(to eat)*	Correr *(to run)*	Leer *(to read)*
Yo	com**o**	corr**o**	le**o**
Tú	com**es**	corr**es**	le**es**
Él / Ella	com**e**	corr**e**	le**e**
Nosotros / Nosotras	com**emos**	corr**emos**	le**emos**
Usted	com**e**	corr**e**	le**e**
Ustedes	com**en**	corr**en**	le**en**
Ellos / Ellas	com**en**	corr**en**	le**en**

Even though is another group and rules, they are not totally different from the first group rules.

In the first group you find structures like "cant**ar**/cant**o**". In the second group this will remain the same, the letter "o" at the end of the "base", for the pronoun "Yo".

For the next pronouns, is not that different either. With the same verb "cant**ar**", you find a conjugation like "él cant**a**" or "nosotros cant**amos**". In the second group that "**a**" practically becomes an "**e**". For example, "él cant**a**" (for cant**ar**) and "él com**e**" (for com**er**). Not very different at all.

Another interesting behavior, compared with the first group rules, is that the conjugation for "él/ella" and "usted" will remain the same. And this will happen with no matter the group.

And it will be the similar situation with the plurals "ustedes" and "ellos/ellas", same conjugation always. Let's practice with these sentences.

But the second group is also a "tricky" one, this because even when knowing that they will have the same rule, most of these words will slightly change, which means that when learning a new second group verb, you have to check the way you should conjugate it.

Here's a small list of **5 common irregular verbs.**

Personal Pronoun	hacer *(to do)*	tener *(to walk)*	Poder *(may/can)*	Querer (to want)	Saber (to know)
Yo	ha**go**	ten**go**	pue**do**	quie**ro**	sé
Tú	hac**es**	tien**es**	pued**es**	quier**es**	sab**es**
Él / Ella	hac**e**	tien**e**	pued**e**	quier**e**	sab**e**
Nosotros / Nosotras	hac**emos**	ten**emos**	pod**emos**	quer**emos**	sab**emos**

Usted	hace	tiene	**puede**	quiere	sabe
Ustedes	hace**n**	tiene**n**	**pueden**	quiere**n**	sabe**n**
Ellos / Ellas	hace**n**	tiene**n**	**pueden**	quiere**n**	sabe**n**

> You can check that all of those verbs have small changes. Although they will keep a similar behavior, "o" for "yo", all the verbs ending with "s" for "tú".
>
> Same conjugation for "él/ella", "usted" and "ustedes", "ellos/ellas"
>
> And the letters "emos" for "nosotros".
>
> So, there's an easy way to master this group, remember the rule, and check how each verb base changes. You now have the 5 most common verbs in this group and 3 others!

Third Group "-ir"

In this group, we basically find the most common verb, but it's at the same time the "king" of the irregular verbs. It's *"to go"* which in Spanish is **"ir"**.

In the third group, we find a couple of verbs which will have a different rule. Although, they won't be much different from the verbs from the second group. And those are good news!

To complete this information, the majority of this verbs will be conjugated in the same way, some have tiny differences but they will become easy to understand once you learn or practice with a couple of them.

➢ **Conjugation rules for third group:**

Personal Pronoun	<u>Viv**ir**</u> *(to live)*	Escrib**ir** *(to write)*	Abr**ir** *(to open)*
Yo	viv**o**	escrib**o**	abr**o**
Tú	viv**es**	escrib**es**	abr**es**
Él / Ella	viv**e**	escrib**e**	abr**e**
Nosotros / Nosotras	viv**imos**	escrib**imos**	abr**imos**
Usted	viv**e**	escrib**e**	abr**e**
Ustedes	viv**en**	escrib**en**	abr**en**
Ellos / Ellas	viv**en**	escrib**en**	abr**en**

As explained before, these similar structures will happen with every verb from every group and also for every tense.

Another interesting fact is that the rules for conjugating these verbs, is not that different from the second group verbs.

For example: "com**en**"   "viv**en**" or "corro"   "abro".

The only small difference would be regarding "nosotros" for which the conjugation will be different.

For example: "com**emos**"   "viv**imos**" or "corr**emos**" "abr**imos**".

Basically it's an "imos" instead of a "emos" from the second group

But then we have a couple of verbs in this group that become irregular when conjugating. It's the case, for example, of **the verb "ir"** which as explained before, it's very irregular and it's Spanish for *"to go"*. **Here's how it's conjugated:**

Personal Pronoun	**Ir** *(to go)*
Yo	**voy**
Tú	**vas**
Él / Ella	**va**
Nosotros / Nosotras	**vamos**
Usted	**va**
Ustedes	**van**
Ellos / Ellas	**van**

As you can see, this time, the verb loses completely its base, creating a new structure in which the letter "v" becomes the new main form. **Good news is** that this only happens with this verb. **No other verb in Spanish will change this much.**

Exercise 1: Complete the following sentences by using the right conjugation for each pronoun and verb group.

a. Daniel _____ (terminar) la tarea / *Daniel finishes the homework.*

b. El perro _____ (vivir) aquí / *The dog lives here.*

c. La casa _____ (tener) dos ventanas / *The house has two Windows.*

d. Yo _____ (querer) un chocolate / *I want a chocolate.*

e. Nosotros _____ (ir) al cine / *We go to the movies.*

f. Usted _____ (escribir) mucho / *You write a lot.*

g. Ellos _____ (comer) ensalada / *They eat salad.*

h. Ustedes _____ (hablar) en inglés / *You (guys) speak in English.*

Part II: Sentences: Affirmative, Negative and Interrogative Form

It is very easy to change between affirmative and negative form in Spanish as the presence of auxiliary verbs "do/did/have/had…" as tools to change between negative, affirmative or even interrogative form, is inexistent. The simple use of "Sí/No" to answer or negate a sentence is good enough. Let's see how it works:

➢ **Affirmative sentences:** an affirmative sentence is a structure in which the idea is expressed or validated as true, real and/or assertive. For example: "You like pizza" is an affirmative sentence as it explains a true fact or validates the idea that in this case, you like something. **In Spanish this happens the same way** and the structure becomes easier as it doesn't need auxiliary verbs to validate, deny or interrogate an idea.

Examples:
María has two kids / **"María tiene 3 hijos"**

Quiero viajar a España / **"I want to travel to Spain"**

The difference between English/Spanish in these sentences is zero. You can see that the position of the words "Noun + verb + complement" is the same in both situations.

On the other hand, in English, you can use "do" to emphasize an idea like "I **do** like pizza" in which ***"do"*** works as an auxiliary verb to "intensify" the fact of liking the pizza. But in Spanish this tool doesn't exist, which means that, to emphasize an idea, you need to use a different word such as an adverb like "really" or "a lot", or words like "of course I do" to highlight or add an intensifier to your idea.

Example:

Conversation 1:

Conversation 2:

This rule won't change regardless the verb, tense or situation. The use of alternative words/tools to emphasize an idea is the way you can create affirmative sentences or answer questions in Spanish.

> **Negative sentences:** on the contrary, a negative sentence is a structure that explains the falsity or unreality of ideas. In Spanish, only by using the adverb "no" is enough to create a sentence in negative form. As explained before, the uses of auxiliary verbs in Spanish, are not to change into negative, affirmative or interrogative form. Check these examples:

Examples:
I don't want to go / **"Yo no quiero ir"**
You don't live in Japan / **"Tú no vives en Japón"**
He can't travel / **"Él no puede viajar"**
She doesn't like pizza / **"A ella no le gusta la pizza"**

On these 4 examples you can check how "no" is the main word to deny to change the ideas into their negative forms. The position of the adverb "no" in a negative sentence for simple tenses in Spanish will be always: noun + **no** + verb + complement.

To summarize this point, we can establish a few points:

- The auxiliary verb is not used to create sentences. Instead, it's only used to create tenses such as the perfect tenses for example.
- In other to emphasize an idea, you have to appeal to different words such as "really, of course, not really…"
- To deny or change any verb into negative form, you only need to place "no" before the verb.

> **Interrogative form:** In Spanish, the interrogative form, and the way you can answer, works in a different way. In this structure you can find the inexistence of auxiliary verb like "*to do*" to create an interrogative sentence or answers such as "*Yes I do/No I don't.*"

Instead, Spanish will only use a single verb to ask the question without the use of any other auxiliary verb. Let's give them a look:

Examples:

Read these short conversations to see how you can ask and answer questions in Spanish. (The main verbs will be highlighted in a question/answer and the translations will be placed next to the bubbles for practical use)

Conversation 1: Casual conversation

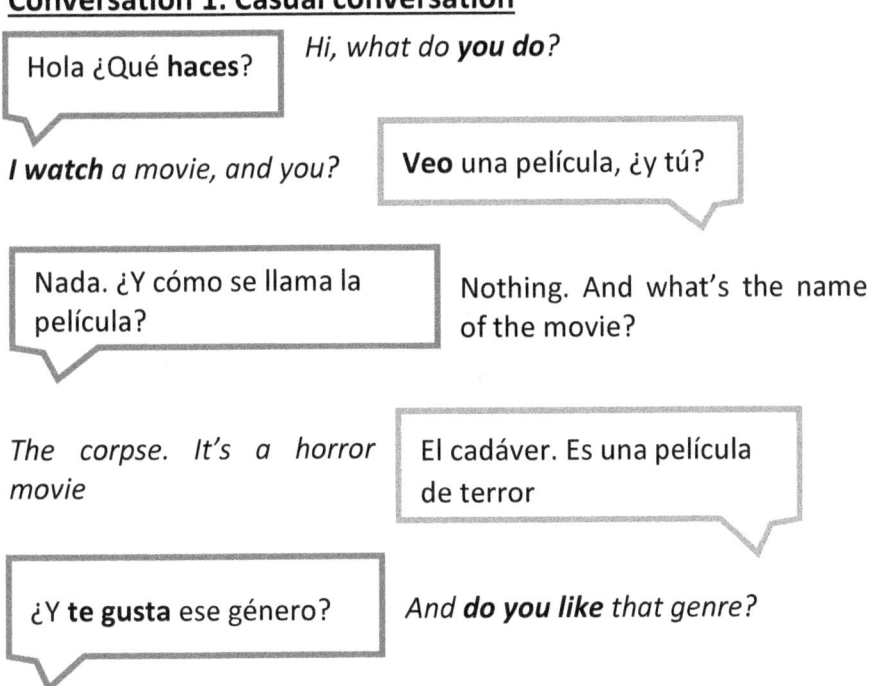

Hola ¿Qué **haces**?

Hi, what do **you do**?

I watch a movie, and you?

Veo una película, ¿y tú?

Nada. ¿Y cómo se llama la película?

Nothing. And what's the name of the movie?

The corpse. It's a horror movie

El cadáver. Es una película de terror

¿Y **te gusta** ese género?

And **do you like** that genre?

Yes, I do. A lot. Sí. Muchísimo

Conversation 2: Casual conversation

Maria, ¿**quieres** un chocolate? *Maria, **do you want** a chocolate?*

¡Claro! *Of course!*

Conversation 3: Casual conversation

***Can you** come today?* ¿**Puedes** venir hoy?

No, I can't. No, no puedo

¿Por qué? *Why?*

Porque estoy enfermo. *Because I feel sick*

⚠️ So, there's no translation for "do" as an auxiliary verb. And as you could notice, Spanish questions are between two question mark "¿?" This is very useful when reading, the person knows a question will be asked. This also happens with exclamation mark "¡!". One opens "¡" and the other "!" closes the sentence.

Even though it would be a grammar error not to use the two marks, any reader will understand if for example you're sending a casual text and you only use one mark at the end of the sentence, as in English.

About answers:

o A simple "Sí" or "No" would be enough to answer a question. You don't need structures like "I do/I don't" or "I can / I can't"
o As any other language, you have additional ways to answer, for example: "Claro/Of course"

> **Interrogative Particles:** About these words such as "what", "how", "why" … There's no further explanation than just a simple translation for each word and two or three little details you have to have in mind when using them. Let's see:
  o **"Qué"**: It means *"what"* in situations like *"what time is it?"* / **"¿Qué hora es?"**, "What *happens?"/* **"¿Qué pasa?"** or *"What do you want?"* / **"¿Qué quieres?"** and many others. It doesn't work for specific situations like *"What's your name?"*. In that case you have to say **"¿Cuál es tu nombre?"**. So that *"what"* becomes **"Cuál"** in Spanish.
  o **"Cuál/Cuáles"**: they can mean *"what"* in some very specific situations like *"what's your name"* or a accurate translation is "Which". Now, the difference between the two words in Spanish is if it's singular or plural.

💡 **But when to use "qué" or "cuál"?** Here are a couple of conditions:

1. "¿Cuál?" and "¿Qué?" when you have or you want to suggest a choice.

In that case you can use **¿Cuál + verb or preposition?** or **¿Qué + noun?**

- ¿Cuál de las tres casas te gusta? / *Which of the three houses you like?*
- ¿Cuál de las dos camisas quieres? / Which of the two shirts do you want?

Or…

- ¿Qué casa es más cara? / Which house is more expensive?
- ¿Qué camisa quieres? / Which shirt do you want?

Both can be used for the same purpose, but as you can see, it's the structure of the sentence that will change when using whether "cuál" or "qué".

2. ¿Qué + verb? to ask for definitions

You can use this form when asking for information or the meaning of things.

- ¿Qué dices? / What do you say?
- ¿Qué significa "saco"? / What does "saco" mean?
- ¿Qué es esto? / What's this?

3. ¿Qué + verb...? / ¿Cuál + verb...? to talk about preferences

In this situation they can be followed by verbs such as "**preferir**/to prefer", "gustar", "querer" ... and the meaning would be the same: suggest choices.

- **¿Qué prefieres, el rock o el jazz?** / What do you prefer, rock or jazz?
- **¿Cúales zapatos te gustan?** / Which shoes do you like?

So, there are few situations when **"Qué"** or **"Cuál"** have a unique use. For the rest of them, feel free to switch from one to the other but just remember how the structure goes.

- **"¿Por qué?"**: it means *"why?"* and it's basically used the same way as in English. To answer a question with this word, you have to use **"Porque"** which is *"because"*.

Example Check these short conversations to see how "por qué/porque" is used in Spanish.

Conversation 1: Giving reasons

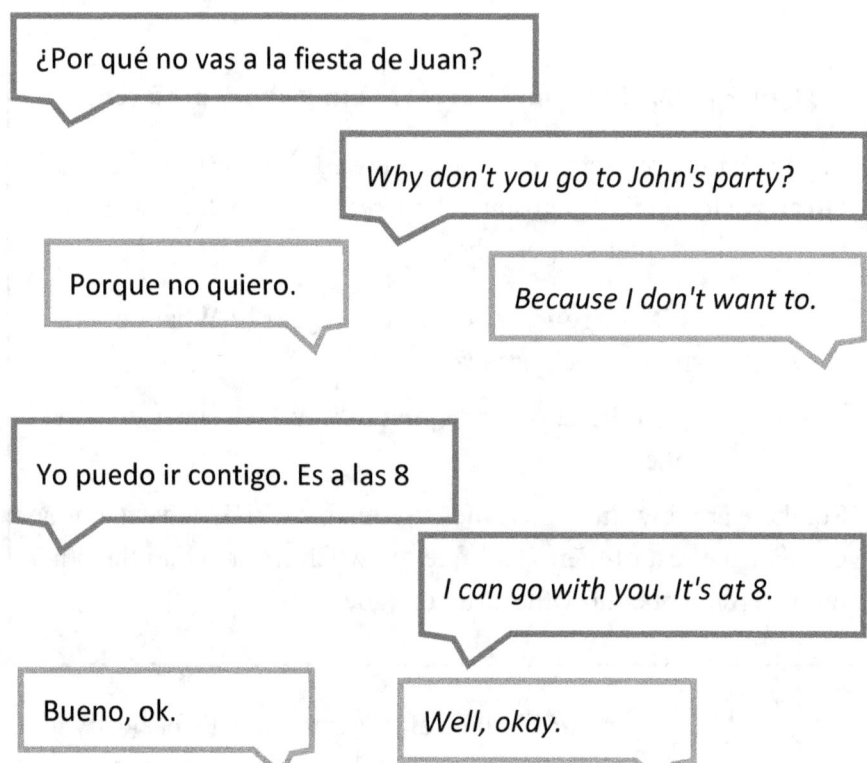

Conversation 2: Casual conversation

- **"¿Cómo?":** it means *"how?"* and it's basically also used the same way as in English. Here are some examples:

    "How are you?" / **"¿Cómo estás?"**
    "How is this possible"? / **"¿Cómo es esto posible?"**

But there are always exceptions. One of them is about the question *"What's your name?"* for which you can use the translated form "¿Cuál es tu nombre?".

But in addition, remember that the common form/verb for asking someone's name is "Llamarse" and in that structure the question would be:

¿Cómo te llamas? *Which would literally be* **How are you called?**

The second exception would be when how is part of an exclamatory sentence. In that case is not translated with the same word in Spanish. Example:

"How amazing!" / **"¡Qué increíble!"**
"How difficult!" / **"¡Qué difícil!"**
"How easy!" / **"¡Qué fácil!"**

So, in these cases, the word "qué" is the one who will be used in Spanish when using exclamatory sentences.

- **"¿Quién?":** it means *"Who?"* and it's used to ask for someone's or something's identity. The only difference -compared to English- is that this particle will have a plural form when the situation requires. Here are the examples:

    "Who are you?" / **"¿Quién eres tú?"**

    "Who's your friend?" / **"¿Quién es tu amigo?"**
    "Who are these people?" / **"¿Quiénes son estas personas?**
    "Who are the invited to the party?" / **"Quiénes son los invitados a la fiesta?"**

The form "Quiénes" will be used when asking the identity of more than one thing. Good news is, there are no exceptions for this particle.

- **"¿Cuándo?":** this is Spanish for *"When?"*. It is used as in English and there are no exceptions. Check the examples:

    "¿Cuándo es la fiesta?" / **"When is the party?"**
    "¿Cuándo vienes?" / **"When do you come?"**
    "¿Cuándo vas a España?" / **"When do you go to Spain?"**

- **"¿Dónde?":** this means *"Where?"*. Here are some examples:

    "Where do you live?" / **"¿Dónde vives?"**
    "Where's the party" / **"¿Dónde es la fiesta?"**

Remember, as in any other language, quick answers are possible and there's no need to give the full answer adding complement and any other excessive information unless you want to be emphatic.

Also remember, the structures "Yes, I do/No I don't" can be translated as simple "Sí/No" without adding any other verb.

Part III: Verb "Gustar"

> This is very interesting verb in Spanish because it doesn't work the same way as in English and it actually makes part of a different group of verbs in this language.
>
> In Spanish, the slightly complex but real explanation is that "gustar" is not a reflexive or regular verb, it needs an object pronoun to be fully conjugated.

The reason is because, while in English this action that affects another noun, in Spanish is totally the opposite. For example: the sentence *"I like pizza"* explains that you have a feeling for the pizza, the action affects the object in the same way you say "I like you"; which means that your feeling "liking" is related to someone. To complete this idea, in this situation "like" is not affecting *you*, is affecting something or someone else.

On the contrary, in Spanish, it needs an object pronoun and a different structure because, literally, something or someone will create on you, the feeling of "liking". Therefore, in a common situation: it can't be reflexive, it doesn't use personal pronouns -it uses a different type called *"prepositional pronouns"* or "pronombres tónicos" and it's also preceded by an object pronoun; thus, it can't be conjugated with the same rules you learned above in this book. As a last detail, in a common situation, it only has two forms: singular and plural.

Here's its structure:

Prepositional Pronoun	Object Pronoun	**Gustar** *(like 1 thing)*	**Gustar** *(like +1 thing)*
A mí	me	**gusta**	gustan
A ti	te	**gusta**	gustan
A él / A ella	le	**gusta**	gustan
A nosotros(as)	nos	**gusta**	gustan
A usted	le	**gusta**	gustan
A ustedes	les	**gusta**	gustan
A ellos / ellas	les	**gusta**	gustan

As you can see, the full composition of this conjugation is composed by 3 parts:

"A prepositional pronoun + An object pronoun + the conjugated form of the verb"

Also, see that the conjugated form of the verb is exactly the same for every single pronoun.

This because you are not "doing" the action, but the action is "affecting" you. Thus, the verb is not directly conjugated with the personal pronoun. And

<u>When you like more than one thing, the verb changes into its plural form "gusta**n**"</u>

Let's check these conversations to have a clearer idea about the way this verb is used:

Conversation 1: Casual conversation

Context: Mario has some *empanadas* a typical Latin-American food, he offers some to his friend Patricia.

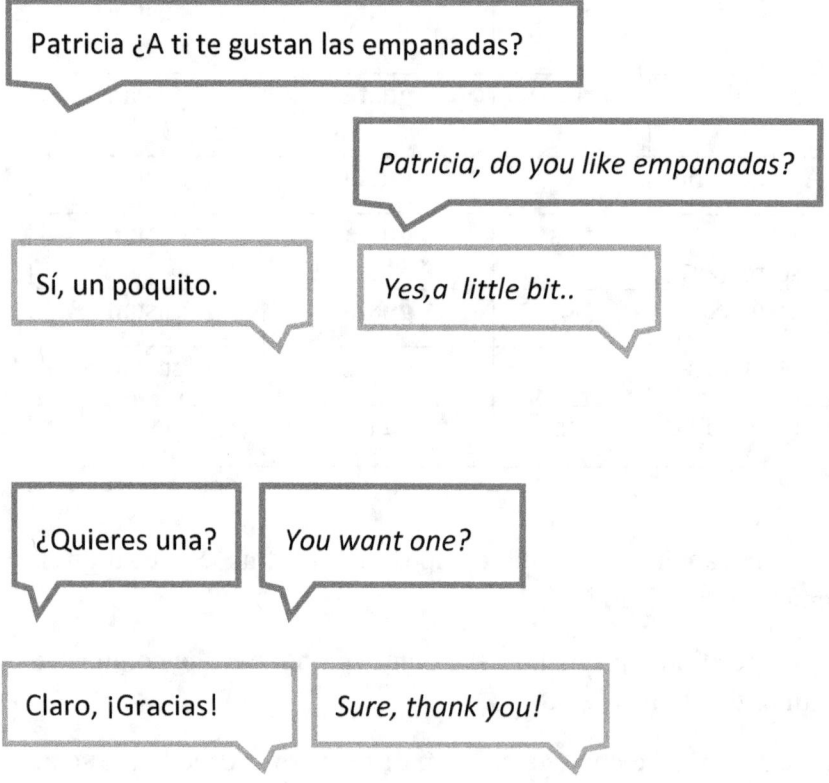

Conversation 2: Casual conversation

Context: Ana is listening a song; she asks Pedro to listen to it.

Conversation 3: Talking about hobbies

¿A ti qué te gusta?

What do you like??

Pues, me gusta cantar ¿y a ti?

Well, I like to sing and you?

A mí me gusta comer.

I like to eat.

A mí también. ¿y qué no te gusta hacer?

Me too. And what don't you like to do?

No me gusta cocinar. ¿Y a ti?

I don't like cooking. And you?

No me gusta ver películas de terror.

I don't like watching horror movies.

A mí tampoco :(

Either do I :(

Conversation 4: Casual conversation

Context: María and Cristina are in the park, Cristina is with her sons and María hasn't know their names

¿Ellos son tus hijos?

Are they your children?

Sí, Juana y Andrés

Yes, Juana and Andres

¿Y qué les gusta?

And what do they like?

Bueno, a Andrés le gusta jugar videojuegos

Well, Andres likes to play video games

¿Y a Juana?

What about Juana?

A Juana le gusta aprender idiomas.

Juana likes to learn languages.

¡Genial! ¡Qué interesante!

That's great! How interesting!

⚠️ From these conversations, we can extract 4 important things which you have to remember or practice when using this verb:

- If there's a noun like food, animals, objects… they have to be preceded by an indefinite article: "Me gustan **las** empanadas" / *I like empanadas.*

- Because this is something or someone that causes a feeling on you, a noun can be placed before the verb: "**Esa canción** me gusta mucho"

- When you're talking about hobbies or activities you like to do, the "action" will be always structured as an infinitive verb: "Me gusta **comer**"

- When talking about other people, the structure is "A + name + le gusta". For example: "A Juan le gusta", "A Andrés le gusta"…

To complete the idea of this verb, in a very unique situation, it can be conjugated as a first-group verb, working as a reflexive verb. It this case, it has a different meaning. When you conjugate this verb like that, it means *"I like myself"* for example. So, pay attention to it. You don't want to sound a bit narcissist. Check the difference with these two sentences:

"**Me gusta la pizza**" / *I like pizza*

"**Me gusto mucho**" / *I like myself a lot.*

As you can see, conjugating this verb with the common rules, will totally change the meaning of your idea in a common situation

If you are in a romantic situation and you want to talk about liking someone, this verb will be conjugated with the pronoun of the person you like. Remember that this verb explains that something or someone causes a feeling on you. Check these last examples:

"**Tú me gustas**" / I like you

"**Ella me gusta**" / She likes me

"**¿Yo te gusto?**" / Do I like you?

Check the structure. The verb is conjugated -following the order of the examples- with "Tú", "Ella" and "Yo" and, in Spanish, these are placed at the beginning because they are doing the action on you, and not on the contrary, like in English. Remember all of these important behaviors!

Try to practice with these exercises:

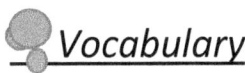
Vocabulary

Within this vocabulary you will find practical words for daily life which will come handy when speaking Spanish, they are divided into 2 categories: activities and food. Try to put them in practice!

Activities	*Food*
"Reading" / "**Leer**"	"Meat" / "**Carne**"
"Listening" / "**Escuchar**"	"Chicken" / "**Pollo**"
"Watching"/"**Mirar**"	"Vegetables" / "**Vegetales**"
"Walking" / "**Caminar**"	"Fish" / "**Pescado**"
"Learning" / "**Aprender**"	"Cheese" / "**Flaco(a)**"
"Doing sports" / "**Hacer ejercicio**"	"Jam" / "**Jamón**"
"To sleep" / "**Dormir**"	"Bread" / "**Pan**"
"Playing" / "**Jugar**" /"Tocar" (when it's an instrument)	"Juice" / "**Jugo**"

Exercise 1: Translate the following sentences into Spanish.

a. *I like reading*

b. *Do you like vegetables?*

c. *Maria likes fish*

d. *He likes to sleep*

e. *I like doing sports*

f. *Juan likes meat*

g. *I like you*

h. *I like myself*

To close this point, here are some **verbs that work the same way as "gustar"** but they are different in "intensity".

Verb (in spanish)	Translation	Example
Encantar	It's understood as "really liking something or someone"	"I really like beaches" / "**Me encantan las playas**"
Fascinar	to cause fascination	"**Me fascinan las pizzas**"

About loving, it exists in Spanish as "amar" but it doesn't work the same way as "gustar" or the previous verbs. In most of the cases, it works as a regular verb with no prepositional or object pronoun. Check this first situation:

"I love pizza" / **"Yo amo las pizzas"**

"I love Spanish / **"Yo amo el español"**

"I love my family / **"Yo amo a mi familia"**

"I love María" / **"Yo amo a María"**

When you are talking about loving something, it works similar to English: "noun + verb + complement", the only difference is the article before the "object" you love. E.g. "Yo amo **las** pizzas"

When it's about loving someone you name, like "family", "María" … You have to use the preposition "a" after the verb. E.g. "Yo amo **a** María".

On the other hand, when you want to directly use a pronoun to replace someone, there's a small difference. Check these examples:

"I love you" / **"Yo te amo"**

"She loves me" / **"Ella me ama"**

"You don't love me" / **"Tú no me amas"**

When this is the case, there's an object pronoun that shows up, "**Te** amo", "**Me** ama", "No **me** amas". This because in Spanish, when doing something to someone, it will require an object pronoun to indicate that the action is affecting someone else.

Part IV: Copulative Verbs "Ser" and "Estar"

> A copulative verb is a word/verb that joins or connects a noun with an adjective or another noun. In Spanish, there are only 3 copulative verbs: "ser", "estar" and "parecer".
>
> In this part of the book you will learn how to use "ser/estar" which in Spanish means "to be". But since there are two translations for the same verb in English, they need to be explained carefully and they require practice.

Let's start with "ser". First, here's its conjugation.

> ➢ **<u>Copulative verb "ser"</u>:** this verb is used for different situations, and identifying each one of them, will make easier use it in the correct way.

First, this is how you conjugate the verb "ser":

Personal Pronoun	<u>**Ser**</u> *(To be)*
Yo	**soy**
Tú	**eres**
Él / Ella	**es**
Nosotros / Nosotras	**somos**
Usted	**es**
Ustedes	**son**
Ellos/Ellas	**son**

It's an irregular verb as you can see and it's used for different situations. Here's a wide list. Learning and practicing this will help you avoid confusion when using this verb.

- **Identity:** this includes a wide list (name, nationality, physical appearance or characteristics, religion and profession) **The use of this verb is understood as something you can never change, or at least not in a short term** like being fat and then skinny or being part of some religion and then turn into some other.

    Examples:
    a. Kombutu is african / **"Kombutu es africano"**
    b. I am José / **"Yo soy José"**
    c. He is catholic / **"Él es católico"**
    d. You are tal / **"Tú eres alto"**
    e. She is an engineer / **"Ella es ingeniera"**
    f. The weather is nice here / **"El clima es bueno aquí"** (In this specific situation, the person wants to explain that the weather is *always* "nice")

- **Family bonds:** this keeps the same principle, a family bond is something you can't change, thus, when explaining "who's who" in your family, you have to use the verb "ser".

    Examples:
    a. Juan and María are my siblings / **"Juan y María son mis hermanos"**
    b. She is my mom / **"Ella es mi mamá"**
    c. I'm his father / **"Yo soy su papá"**

- **Time:** verb "ser" is used when talking about time, date and seasons.

    Examples:
    a. Today is Monday / **"Hoy es lunes"**
    b. It's 10:15 / **"Son las 10:15"**
    c. It's January / **"Es enero"**
    d. It's summer / **"Es verano"**
    e. The party is tomorrow / **"La fiesta es mañana"**

- **Price**

    Examples:
    -How much is it? / **"¿Cuánto es?"**
      -It's 60 / **"Son 60"**

- **The origin of something/someone:** in this specific point it could be about nationality or the materials used to craft something.

    Examples:
    a. I'm from Peru / **"Yo soy de Perú"**
    b. Where are you from? / **"¿De dónde eres tú?**
    c. A gold ring / **"Un anillo de oro"**

To summarize this point, we can establish that:

The meaning of this verb is generally used to express identity, and it makes sense for all of the examples, even when talking about price, because a price is a value you can't change that fast. Or also about the day or time, it's the identity of the day, we named them to identify them and that's why they use "ser".

You can remember these situations and keep this "meaning" in mind, and it will become easier to use it in daily life.

> **Copulative verb "estar"**: this verb is used for different situations, and identifying each one of them, will make easier to use it in the correct way.

First, this is how you conjugate the verb "estar":

Personal Pronoun	**Estar** *(To be)*
Yo	**Estoy**
Tú	**Estás**
Él / Ella	**está**
Nosotros / Nosotras	**estamos**
Usted	**está**
Ustedes	**están**
Ellos/Ellas	**Están**

This one is an irregular verb too, and it's used for totally different situations from those in which you would use "ser". Check this wide list of cases that need the use of "estar":

- **Location:** basically, this verb explains or make reference to temporary situations, facts or things that will not remain in the same state as time passes. So, when you want to explain that you are in a place, you have to use this verb, even if the place you're living is the place you will live forever in. The verb "ser" won't be used ever for a situation in which locations are involved, why? Because you can't identify someone or something using a location in Spanish. Check these examples:

    Examples:
    a. Where are you? / "**¿Dónde estás tú?**"
    b. I'm in Costa Rica / "**Yo estoy en Costa Rica**"
    c. Are you at home? / "**¿Estás en casa?**"
    d. Yes, I'm here / "**Sí, estoy aquí**"

- **Feelings/Mood/State of mind/Status:** all of these points are related, they all have one thing in common, the temporary meaning. Read the following conversations to have a clearer idea.

Conversation 1: Asking for a direction

Context: Manuel ask someone where's the train station

Conversation 2: A bit of geography

Context: Juan is texting his friend Alberto. Alberto likes to travel the world and he is always visiting new countries and culture

> Alberto, ¿en qué parte del mundo estás?

> Alberto, where in the world are you?

> En Perú, es un país en el centro de Latinoamérica

> In Peru, it is a country in the center of Latin America

> ¡Qué cool! ¿Y cómo es la gente allá?

> How cool! And how's the people there?

> La gente es muy amable

> The people are very friendly

> ¿qué tal la comida?

> How's the food?

> ¡Es una maravilla!

> Marvelous!

¿Y cuál es tu próximo destino?

And what's your next destination?

Voy a Argentina y luego a México

I go to Argentina and then to Mexico

¡México es mi país favorito!

Mexico is my favorite country!

Conversation 3: Planning to go out

Context: Juan and María are planning to go out because they are bored.

Conversation 4: About food

Context: María made some burritos, she then offers one to Juan

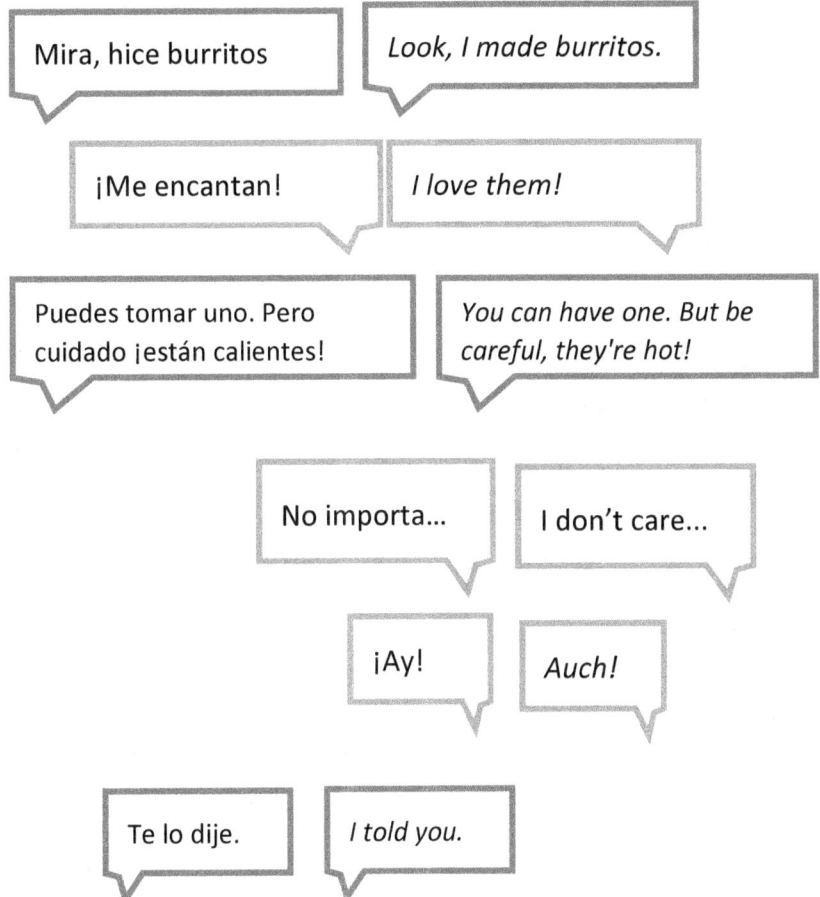

These two verbs meet the grammar requirement according to each situation. But also, Spanish speakers can understand them as the meaning they have and sometimes, you might find situations in which you can ask yourself *"why "ser" and not "estar"?* And the answer will always have a logical sense. When practicing with some exercises, you might find adverbs like "now", "already", "yet", "in a while" to complete the idea of being a temporary or permanent situation. But in real life, these are not needed or they are not mandatory because using either "ser" or "estar" will give context to the sentence.

In any case, here are a couple of situations in which "ser" and "estar" only change the sense of the idea.

Sentence in English	Situation with "ser"	Situation with "estar"
I'm skinny	**Soy flaco**	**Estoy flaco**

In this frame you will find two situations which would be translated in English with the same exact form, but in Spanish, the meaning/sense will according to the verb you choose.

Giving the context, let's say someone is saying "I'm skinny" and this person chooses to say **"Soy flaco"**. In that case, this person is not thinking about the rules and how's the best grammar way to explain that. On the contrary, he/she wants to express a meaning. When using "Soy" it means that this person is identifying himself/herself as a skinny person in a "forever" meaning.

On the other hand, when this person chooses to say **"Estoy flaco"**, he/she wants to explain that maybe he/she is feeling skinny or he/she knows or have a certain conviction that this won't be his/her condition forever. He/she might go to the gym, eat a bit more and get some weight. All this context is given only by choosing or switching between "ser" or "estar".

Let's analyze a different situation:

Sentence in English	Situation with "ser"	Situation with "estar"
This is easy	**Esto es fácil**	**Esto está fácil**

This is an interesting situation but it keeps the same logical meaning.

When saying "**El clima es bueno**" it means that, for example, in certain city, the weather is always nice. Sure, sometimes it might rain or sometimes is dry, but the meaning that the person wants to give to his/her idea, is that it remains nice most of the time.

Now, on the contrary, choosing "**estar**" to explain this idea, it would be like in a situation when you wake up in the morning and the sun is shining and the sky is clear and you do like that weather, and you want to express that *now* the weather is nice, and you do know that tomorrow might change or it's not like that always. Just the idea of "today is a nice day". If that's the case, you would say "**El clima está bueno**".

Sentence in English	Situation with "ser"	Situation with "estar"
The weather is nice	**El clima es bueno**	**El clima está bueno**

Let's check one last situation:

With these specific situations, there's a thin and almost invisible wall between the two of them.

The difference here is how do you want to express your idea. **"Esto es fácil"** you want to simply explain that is always easy and you have the ability to solve that situation.

And when using **"Esto está fácil"** it's that you feel that it's easy, you want just to explain that *now* is easy. With these specific cases, when things are easy, difficult, hard... your choice won't affect the meaning, and people will understand the idea without correcting you.

To complete this process, let's practice:

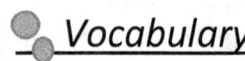 *Vocabulary*

Within this vocabulary you will find practical words for daily life which will come handy when speaking Spanish, they are divided into 2 categories: places and feelings. Try to put them in practice! **Some of the feelings and status have a male and female form, which has to match the gender of the noun.**

Places	*Feelings*	*Status*
"Building" / **"Edificio"**	"Happy" / **"Feliz"**	"Hot" / **"Caliente"**
"Beach" / **"Playa"**	"Sad" / **"Triste"**	"Cold" / **"Frío(a)"**
"School"/**"Escuela"**	"Excited" / **"Emocionado(a)"**	"Warm" / **"Tibio(a)"**
"Square" / **"Plaza"**	"Worried" / **"Preocupado(a)"**	"Boiling" / **"Hirviendo"**
"(At) Work" / **"(En) el trabajo"**	"In love" / **"Enamorado(a)"**	
"Mall" / **"Centro Comercial"**	"Scared" / **"Asustado(a)"**	
"(Super)market" / **"(Super)mercado"**		
"(At) home" / **"(En) casa**		

Exercise 1: Translate the following sentences into Spanish.

a. I'm in Honduras

b. Are you ok?

c. Maria is excited

d. We are in the supermarket

e. Juan is in love

f. I'm in the mall

g. They are at work

h. You are at home

i. It's cold

j. The pizza is hot

Exercise 2: Fill the blanks of the conversations by using the right verb (ser o estar).

Juan: hola Ana ¿Cómo _____ ?
Ana: Bien ¿y tú?
Juan: _____ emocionado
Ana: ¿Por qué?
Juan: porque _____ en Roma.

María: Pedro ¿Dónde _____ ?
Pedro: Yo _____ en la plaza.
María: Dale. Yo voy en 10 minutos. _____ en casa.
Pedro: Bueno, te espero / *I wait for you*

Prepositions

On this subpart of the chapter, you will learn how to translate 3 prepositions to talk about location, these are "in", "on" and "at".

In Spanish, the specification of locations using different prepositions is not relevant. On the contrary, the use of one single word/preposition can explain -by logical context- if the object or person is placed in, on or at some place.

The translation for those three words is **the preposition "en"**.

"En" can explain the location of a noun in the virtual or physical space without the need of specifying if it's on a surface, in a closed space or at a common place.

This means that even the relative, figurative, temporal or grammatical differences such as *"in the house" / "at home"* or *"On July" / "in the morning"* and *"in Jail" / "at Jail"* are not important in Spanish.

In this language, people can understand the idea by being aware of the context or by overexplaining the situation the person is referring to.

For example, if someone tells you *"the keys are on the table"* in Spanish the translation would be **"las llaves están en la mesa"** but "en" could mean "in/on/at" but the most logical context will make the person understand that the keys are *"on top"* of the table and the only or the first place this person will go to search for the keys will be *"on"* the table.

It has to be a table with drawers or a very unusual or unique situation in order to create confusion or a multiple-option situation, but in that case, the person would use a very specific word to explain the exact location of something/someone. Translations for words like *"inside"*, *"on top/above"*. But for the rest of the situations, the same **"en"** will be used and will possess a meaning that will adapt to the context or situation.

Part V: Reflexive Verbs

> In Spanish, the reflexive form of an action - which in English would be understood as those who work together with reflexive pronouns such as "myself" in a sentence like "I watch myself in the mirror" or "I see yourself in the future" – they don't work in the same way.

A reflexive verb can explain that an action is affecting "you" but it is not the case in most of the situations in Spanish.

Instead, a reflexive verb in Spanish goes beyond the uses it has in English and can or have to be used in actions that won't be translated as something you do to "yourself"

Check these examples:

- ➢ "I **eat** sandwich" / "Yo **me como** un sándwich"
- ➢ "You **go** to Madrid" / "Tú **te vas** a Madrid"
- ➢ We **wake up** at 7:00" / "Nosotros **nos levantamos** a las 7:00"

In those examples you can observe that the verb in English is translated differently in Spanish, there's another word which is called "reflexive pronoun" and when it goes with a verb, they form a "reflexive verb" which is Spanish, most of the time is an intransitive verb and the reflexive pronoun is used to make emphasis of the action, to change the target of the verb, or to explain that its result is affecting the person or thing who doing the action.

To complete this idea, even when you find yourself in a situation in English in which you would like or need to use a translation for "by myself", they don't need to use a reflexive pronoun. Instead, it could or has to be a different word.

Read this conversation to have some examples:

Conversation 1: Casual Conversation

Context: two young people talk about where do they live. One of them lives by himself.

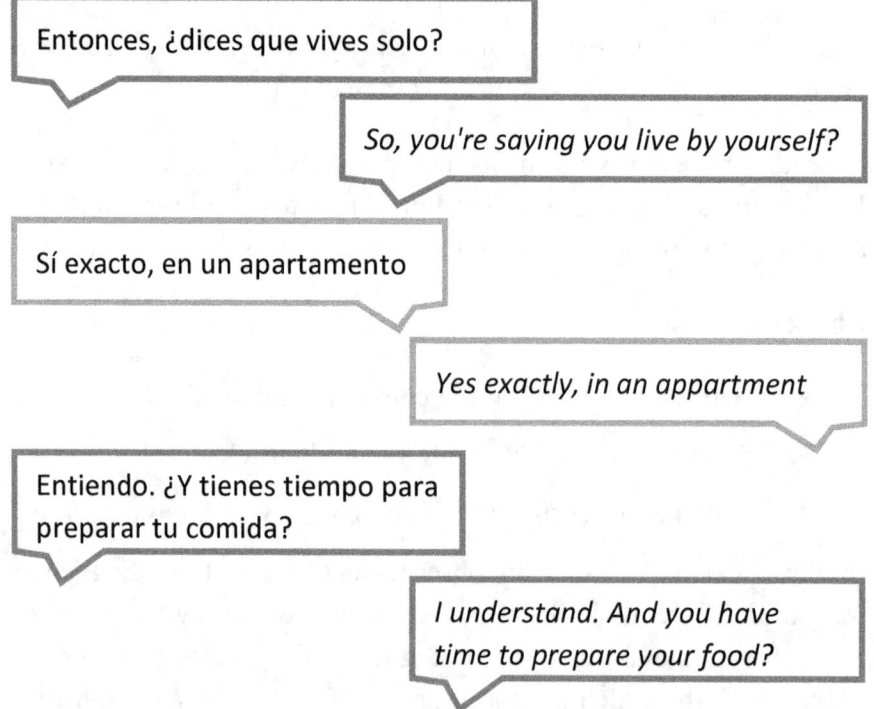

> Es difícil. Pero a veces cocino o si no, ordeno comida a domicilio.

> *It's hard. But sometimes I cook or I order food at home.*

> Claro, debe ser difícil vivir por tu cuenta.

> *Of course, it must be hard to live on your own.*

💡 From this conversation you can obtain two different situations to translate an English reflexive pronoun.

- The translation for *"by yourself"* it's simple and doesn't involve any reflexive pronoun. In fact, **"solo"** means also *"alone"* so literally in Spanish, it's "I live alone".

- The second situation is a synonym of *"by youself/by your own"* which in Spanish can also be **"por tu cuenta"**. Both are most likely used in Spanish.

Conversation 2: Planning a travel

Context: Lola is telling her friend Valentina about her trip to Barcelona next week

> ¿Y te vas con Pedro?
>
> *And you're going with Pedro?*
>
> Sí, nos vamos juntos.
>
> *Yes, we're leaving together.*

💡 In this conversation, if you observe, most of the verb have a reflexive pronoun "**te** vas", "**me** voy", "**me** quiero comer" and specially "querer" and/or "comer" are not translated or understood as *"want myself"* or *"eat myself"*.

This is structure is highly common and understanding this will make your life easier in Spanish. Most of all of the actions can or will have a reflexive pronoun but they won't mean that the action is affecting oneself. Remember there are a couple of uses for reflexive verbs and just one of them is to explain is a reflexive action like in English, but the other cases are to make emphasis or to change the meaning or direction of the verb's action

---

To keep learning about the reflexive verbs, **remember they are actions preceded or followed by a reflexive pronoun** which will make emphasis, change the direction of the action or work as a reflexive situation where the translation will use the structure *"-self"* in English.

On the first pages of this book, you found yourself with the first reflexive verb *"llamarse"* which is the common way to introduce yourself in Spanish. In this specific case, Spanish people understand it as *"I call myself _____ "* because that's basically what name are for "to call yourself" with a word that can give you an identity.

But for other verbs or situations - even though the action makes emphasis on the person or thing who's doing the action – it might be impractical to translate them adding "*-self*" because at the beginning, where you still think in English while speaking in Spanish, it won't make sense to you and you will try to avoid saying actions in a "reflexive" way, which is very common -and correct- in Spanish. But first, let's learn the reflexive pronouns.

Here you can observe the list of the reflexive pronouns in Spanish:

Reflexive Pronouns

Personal Pronoun	Reflexive Pronoun
Yo	**me**
Tú	**te**
Él / Ella	**se**
Nosotros / Nosotras	**nos**
Usted	**se**
Ustedes	**se**
Ellos/Ellas	**se**

On the other hand, **to identify a reflexive verb,** you have to observe its infinitive form. This form will have *"-se"* at the end of the word. This is how a verb changes into its reflexive form. I.e. "llamar**se**", "comer**se**", "bañar**se**", "ir**se**"…

A useful and good way you can practice these verbs is by learning how to explain your daily routine. For these actions, the reflexive verbs will be present to explain that it is you who's doing the action. Check this vocabulary:

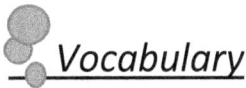
Vocabulary

Within this vocabulary you will find practical words for daily routine which will come handy when speaking Spanish, You can find the conjugation of each verb in the last pages of this book!

Activity	*Translation*
Despertarse/Levantarse	To wake up/To get up
Ir al baño	To go to the bathroom
Bañarse*/Tomar una ducha	To take a shower
Vestirse	To get dressed
Desayunar	To have breakfast
Almorzar	To have lunch
Cenar	To have dinner
Tomar una siesta	To take a nap
Acostarse a dormir	To go to sleep

As you can observe, many of these verbs are reflexive verbs, which means that, when talking or explaining your daily routine, you will need to use a reflexive pronoun for most of those actions.

To include some other points:

- The translation for *"take a shower"* have two options. In the frame, the verb **"bañarse"** has an asterisk because this verb is more commonly used than "tomar una ducha". Most of the time, Spanish speakers will say "me baño" instead of "tomo una ducha". In the end it's free choice but using "bañarse" is a good way to sound natural and practice reflexive verbs.

- The three verbs for food *"have breakfast, lunch and dinner"* work in a different way. They are just one single word/verb. Which means that by conjugating them, you already include the food you are eating/having for each moment of the day. For example: "I **have breakfast**" = "Yo **desayuno**".

    And when the moment comes to explain the food you have/eat, it has to be placed after the conjugation and not in the middle. For example: "I have **sandwich** for breakfast" = Yo desayuno **sandwich**".

Reflexive Verb vs Simple Verb in Daily Life

Another interesting fact is that, even though most of the actions can be switched into regular reflexive form, there is a critical difference when using either of these structures. Read carefully the explanation below to better understand the way you can use the reflexive form of those verbs you can also use in regular form:

> **Reflexive verbs in daily life:** a reflexive action that you can switch it into a regular verb (with no reflexive pronoun) has

or have an article between to avoid an unprecise result when speaking in Spanish. Check these examples:
   a. I drink water in the morning / "Yo me bebo **un vaso de agua** en la mañana"
   b. You read books / "Tú te lees **unos libros**"
   c. Every morning, I prepare coffee / "Cada mañana me preparo **un café**"
   d. I have pizza for lunch / "Me desayuno **una pizza**"

- **Regular verb in daily life:** all of the previous actions you can explain them without adding the reflexive pronoun. In that case, even though it is common to hear people using reflexive pronouns with these actions, sometimes they don't, or sometimes you don't need to either. Now, when that's the case, the use of an article or words to explain what you eat, drink, read… is not necessary. Check these examples:
   a. I drink water in the morning / "Yo bebo **agua** en la mañana"
   b. You read books / "Tú lees **libros**"
   c. Every morning, I prepare coffee / "Cada mañana preparo **café**"
   d. I have pizza for lunch / "Desayuno **pizza**"

Both are 100% correct, and the choice is yours to select which one you would most likely use when speaking Spanish because with these actions, the alternance is possible to explain the same idea. Although, some other verbs can't switch between regular or reflexive form to explain the same.

Remember other of the uses is to change or explain the direction of the action. In this case, the use of a reflexive pronoun explains it's you who's doing the action and not to someone else. Keep reading the next segment to understand this point.

> ### Reflexive verbs with unique meaning or direction: a couple of reflexive verbs can't eliminate their reflexive pronoun and explain the same idea like in the previous examples. These verbs, for example, if it is you who's waking up, the conjugation needs to possess a reflexive pronoun, if not, the sentence would be understood as if you are "waking some else up". So, it is important to identify these verbs and use them in the correct way according to the situations. Here's a small list of the most common verbs that require to be in a reflexive form when the noun is doing the action and this is not affecting anyone else in the sentence:
>   - "Despertarse/Levantarse"
>   - "Bañarse"
>   - "Cepillarse"
>   - "Acostarse"
>   - "Llamarse"
>   - "Vestirse"
>
> The list is just a bit longer than those verbs but you can already recognize those above.
>
> **What happens if they are not in a reflexive form?** The action goes or affect another noun. Observe this comparison:
>
> "Yo **me levanto** a las 7:00" vs. "Yo **levanto a Daniel** a las 7:00"
>
> > The difference between the two actions is -as you might have observed- who's waking up. In the first

sentence it is *"me"* who's waking up, and the verb needs its reflexive pronoun to direct the action onto the noun.

On the contrary, the second sentence is different. In this case the translation is not "Daniel wakes up" but "I wake Daniel up".

"Yo **me baño**" vs "Yo **baño al perro**"

With this comparison, the situation is the similar. In the first translation, It's *"I take a shower"* whereas in the other sentence it's "I bathe the dog". The action changes.

"Yo **me llamo** José" vs "Yo **llamo a José**"

In this last example, you can observe how important is to properly conjugate one of these verbs according to the situation. "Yo me llamo José" means "My name is José" or "I call myself José" which is the way you can introduce yourself in Spanish. On the contrary, the other sentence explains "I call José (on the phone for example)" which is totally different.

⚠️ All of these examples converge into an important fact or rule. An action made by someone and it is affecting someone else, can't have a reflexive pronoun.

"Yo me baño al perro" would be a grammatical error.

The same for actions that require reflexive to explain that they affect the same noun who's doing it.

"Yo llamo José" would be wrong too.

Observe these 3 daily routines to have a clearer idea:

Todos los días me levanto a las 5:00	*Every day I get up at 5:00*
Luego me baño, me visto y desayuno	*Then I take a shower, I get dressed and have breakfast*
Voy al trabajo a las 7:00	*I go to work at 7:00*
Luego almuerzo pizza o pasta	*Then I have pizza or pasta for lunch*
A las 9:00 me acuesto a dormir	*At 9:00 I go to sleep*

Los sábados, a las 7 me levanto y desayuno	*On Saturdays, at 7 I get up and have breakfast*
Luego me baño y me visto	*Then I take a shower and get dressed*
Miro televisión	*I watch TV*
Hago ejercicio	*I exercise*
A las 10 me acuesto a dormir	*At 10 I go to sleep*

Todos los lunes me levanto a las 6	*Every Monday I get up at 6*
Desayuno y me baño	*I eat breakfast and I take a shower*
Luego me visto y voy al trabajo	*Then I get dressed and go to work*
A las 12 almuerzo	*At 12 I have lunch*
A las 7 ceno pizza	*At 7 I have pizza for dinner*
A las 10 me acuesto a dormir	*At 10 I go to sleep*

With these examples you can observe and learn how daily routines are explained in Spanish, some of those actions require reflexive form and some others don't. Try to create your daily routine and explain all the activities you do on a regular day!

Part VI: Deictic Verbs

> A deictic verb is a word that represents an action whose interpretation depends on who is doing it or the sender in a conversation. In Spanish there are 4 of this kind are they are *"ir", "venir", "llevar"* and *"traer"*. They have very specific uses and, on this chapter, you will learn how to put them in a context or conversation.

An interesting fact in Spanish is the consistency of its verbs' meaning. They will always possess a logical use that will remain the same no matter the situation (tense, mood...) They can change their structure and add reflexive forms which will totally modify their meaning, but when talking about these deictic verbs, it is important to understand that they work different from English but because they will hold onto the same rules they naturally have.

For example, "To go" / **"ir"** is a deictic verb. When someone (a sender) explains that another person or thing *"goes"*/ **"va"**. it means that this person will move from the point where the sender is talking, to a different position where the sender is not located. So, moving from point A to B will use a different verb than moving from B to A in Spanish. It all depends on who's doing the action and where this person is going, or coming.

Before moving forward with the examples, you can also have in mind a simple formula to learn this easier: in Spanish, moving to *"here"* and moving to *"there"* can't be explained with the same verb. "Ir" will always have the connotation of "there" and "venir" will possess the meaning of "here".

Also, getting back to the same point you are, will use "venir" and going to a point you've never been at, will use "ir".

An additional tool, for an illustrated explanation can be these diagrams:

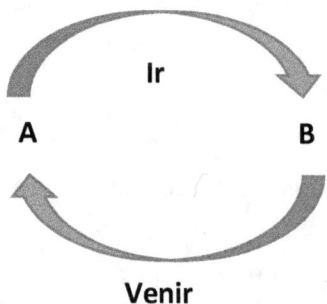

One last information you need is the conjugation of these two irregular verbs:

Personal Pronoun	**Ir** *(To go)*	**Venir** *(To come)*
Yo	**voy**	**vengo**
Tú	**vas**	**vienes**
Él / Ella	**va**	**viene**
Nosotros / Nosotras	**vamos**	**venimos**
Usted	**va**	**viene**
Ustedes	**van**	**vienen**
Ellos/Ellas	**van**	**vienen**

> **Deictic verb "ir":** "to go" in Spanish will be always used when someone moves from point A to B and it doesn't matter how close point B is from point A.

Point "A" is the point in which the sender or the noun who's doing the action is located, if that person or thing moves to a different place where neither the sender or the person/thing are that location is **point "B"**.

In Spanish you will always use "ir" to go from point A to point B. (From the place you are at that moment, to the place you are not at.

Let's say you are at home and you want to go to the kitchen, that's point B, and that displacement you are doing will use **"ir"** in Spanish.

Observe these examples:

A ⟹ B

*María **goes** to the beach with Alejandro* / "María **va** a la playa con Alejandro"

So, in this case María is on point A (wherever the place she is at) and she will move to point B (the beach, the place where she is not at). The simple fact that something or someone moves from a place to another where the sender or the person who's doing the action is not at, that action has to be explained with **"ir"**.

A ⟹ B

*You **go** to the house today* / "Tú **vas** a la casa hoy"

This example might illustrate in a easy way, the idea of **"ir"**. In this case, it's the same, you are on point A and you move to point B (the house).

Now, observe this conversation to have another example with this verb:

Conversation 1: Going to a party

Context: Ana is texting Valentina to see if she wants to go to a party. (None of them are at the party)

💡 So, what's happening? Both are not at the party, and the party is point B.

They are sending messages from different parts, but they are both at point A because they are not at the goal/the party/point B.

And this is critical, no matter if you are in China and a friend is in Alaska, if both are planning to go to a different place where none of you both are, that will be always point B, the destination, the goal.

> **Deictic verb "venir":** the action of this verb explains a displacement, so it is similar with "ir" only in that fact. Now, on the contrary, "venir" will be used only when someone/something is moving from point B to point A. Which means that if the person is talking to you and he/she will move to your location, he/she is on point B and will move to point A. In this case, "venir" is the verb to be used on.

Also, if two people are in the same place, and they are talking about wanting to come back to the same location later, in this case, "venir" will be used too. Why? Because the place is point A and coming back to the same location means that you are moving from a different spot, to this place again, and moving from B to A, requires the use of "venir".

Observe these examples:

B ⟹ A

Tomorrow I ***come (back)*** *to this beach again /* "Mañana **vengo** a esta playa otra vez"

The person is getting back to the same point, when this happens, "venir" will be the verb to put in use.

Can you please come (here) at 7:00? / ¿Puedes por favor **venir** a las 7:00?

This person wants to ask the other person if he/she can get back to the same point.

Now take a look at this conversation:

Conversation 2: At the restaurant

Context: Carlos is talking to Juana at the restaurant. (Both are in the same place)

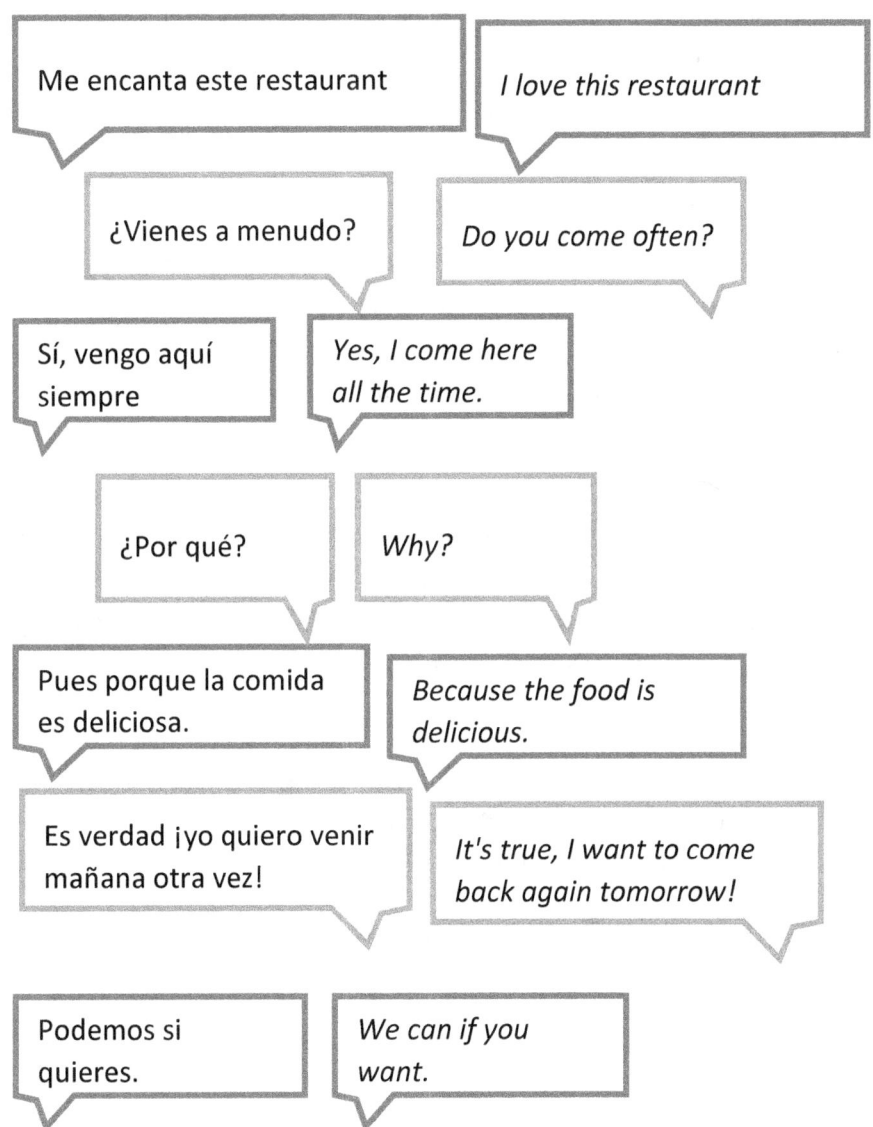

> So, what's happening? Both are not in the same place
>
> In this case getting back to the same place both are at the moment they are speaking, wil require the use of "venir".
>
> If you and your friend are both in China and both will travel to USA but will eventually return to China, the verb "venir" will be needed for that situation.

But what happens when you are talking on the phone with someone and that person tells you to go to his/her place? Then you have to choose the right verb! Let's move forward with *"ir vs. venir"*.

Ir vs. Venir

In English, if you are talking on the phone, which someone and both are in different places, and the person asks you *"Hey, do you come to the party?"* you can answer *"Yes, I'll come"*. Which means that you can answer with the same verb, even though you are in different places. But that won't happen in Spanish.

In Spanish, if someone asks you to get to the same place he/whe is at, this person will use "venir" and you have to answer with "ir" because you are not in the same location.

To illustrate these two differences, observe this conversation:

Conversation 3: Talking on the phone

Context: Juan and Andrés are talking on the phone; Juan is in a party and Andrés is at home. (They are in two different places)

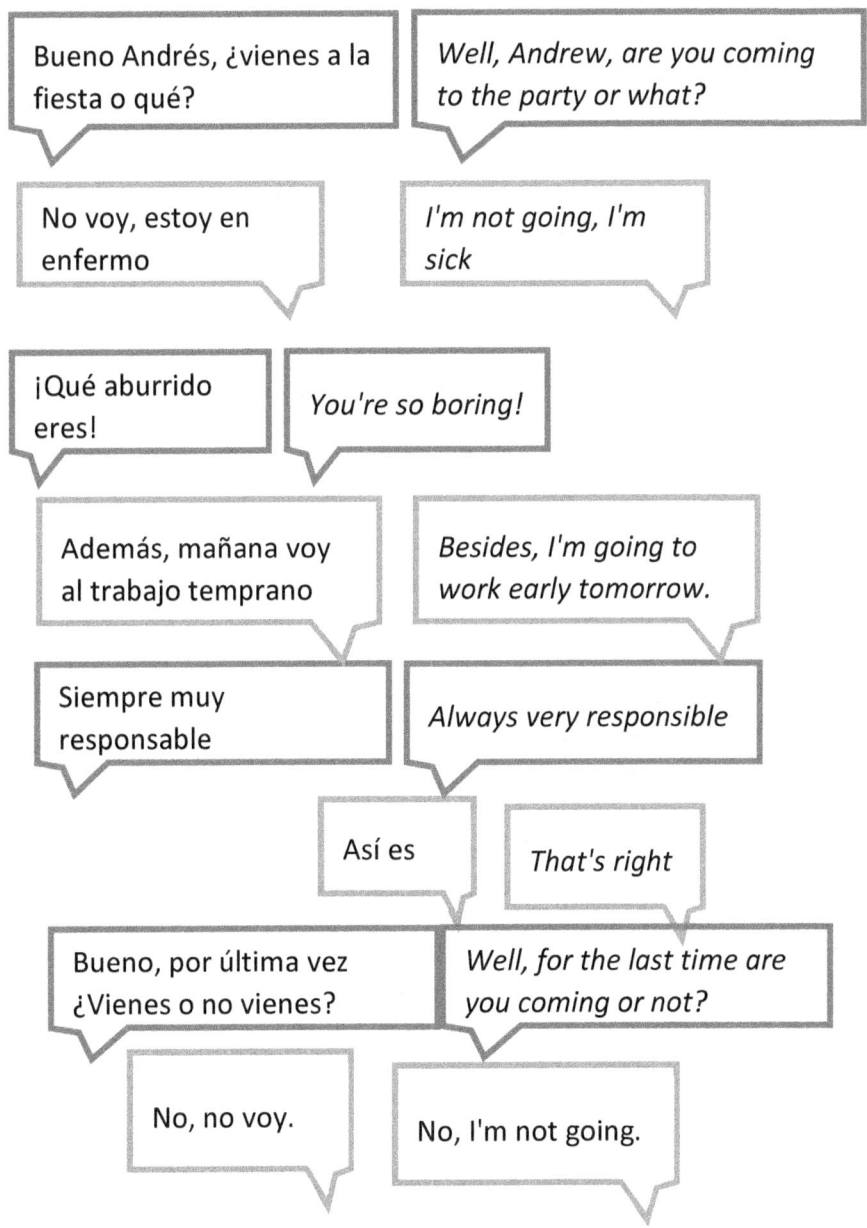

To summarize this point, these verbs are different words for different purposes.

You will always use "ir" if you move to a different place.

> For example: *I go home* / **"voy a casa"**

You will always use "venir" if you get back to the same place you are at the moment you are talking.

> For example: *I buy something and come (back) later* / **"compro algo y vengo más tarde"**

If you talk to someone else about moving to a different place, you use "ir".

> For example: *Do we go to the beach?* / **"¿Vamos a la playa?"**

If you talk to someone else about moving to the place you are at, you use "venir"

> For example: *You come here tomorrow?* / **"¿Vienes aquí mañana?"**

To add more information related to this topic, remember to check the vocabulary at the end of the book

To complete the deictic verbs, remember they are four. You already have the idea about two of them: "ir" and "venir".

The other 2 left are "llevar" and "traer". These verbs are directly related to the two before. This means that the actions of these two new verbs depend on where are you displacing, who's the sender or person talking and the location you are at the moment.

To easier understand or to have greatly accurate idea about these 4 verbs are related, you can remember this rule:

"ir" goes with "llevar" which means if *"tú vas, tú llevas"*

"Venir" goes with "traer" which means if **"tú vienes, tú traes"**

The relationship between each verb is very important and will help you understand their differences with their specific actions and with which would be their translations in English *"to take"* or *"to bring"*.

In English, the verbs *"to take"* and *"to bring"* have a relationship with *"going"* or *"coming"*, but remember those verbs are not used in the same way in Spanish, thus, the same situations where you can used them in English, are not the same in this language you are learning.

Before the explanation, here are the conjugations of these two deictic verbs:

Personal Pronoun	**Llevar** *(To bring <there>)*	**Traer** *(To bring<here>)*
Yo	**voy**	**vengo**
Tú	**vas**	**vienes**
Él / Ella	**va**	**viene**
Nosotros / Nosotras	**vamos**	**venimos**
Usted	**va**	**viene**
Ustedes	**van**	**vienen**
Ellos/Ellas	**van**	**vienen**

Let's move forward with each explanation:

➢ **Deictic verb "llevar"**: this verb explains the action of holding something or someone and deliver this to a different location. (From point A to point B) This action is bounded or tied to "ir, hence, if you want to go to a friend's house and deliver a gift, you will use this action. **Remember "to bring" or "to take" can be used to translate these actions, but have in mind that** *"to bring <here>"* **and** *"to bring <there>"* **are** two different verbs in Spanish. Check these examples:

*I go to the party and I **bring** two friends* / "Voy a la fiesta y **llevo** dos amigos"

> 💡 This short sentence shows an action in which the person goes to a place (point B) and he/she will get there with two friends, and because the verb **"to bring"** in this situation is related to **"to go"** in Spanish the only option you have is to use **"llevar"**

> ⚠️ A critical fact is that **"to take"** in English can be used in two situations basically: as a synonym for **"to pick"** which is related to the action of holding something with your hand which would be released at some point in time-space, and the second would be for example when you take a taxi and you ask the driver to take you to a different place.
>
> In Spanish **"to take"** only has one translation **"tomar/coger"** and one meaning: as a synonym of **"to pick"** or the action of holding something with you.
>
> For example: *"take this gift, is for you"* / **"toma este regalo, es para ti"**
>
> If it's an example related to taking a taxi, the translation is different.
>
> For example: *"can you take me to the beach?"* / **"¿puedes llevarme a la playa?"**
>
> **"llevar"** is the verb because you are displacing from point A (the taxi) to point B (the beach)
>
> **"Tomar"** is not a verb you can relate to displacement in Spanish; thus, it can't be used in this situation.

➢ **Deictic verb "traer":** this verb, talking about displacement, is totally the opposite of **"llevar"**. Remember this action is strictly related to **"venir"**, so the action of bringing or holding something you will deliver to a place, has to be from point B to point A. Observe this conversation:

Conversation 1: In the office

Context: Juan is in the office and he's talking to his friend José - who's also in the same place- Juan is telling that tomorrow is his birthday and they are planning about what to bring to the office tomorrow.

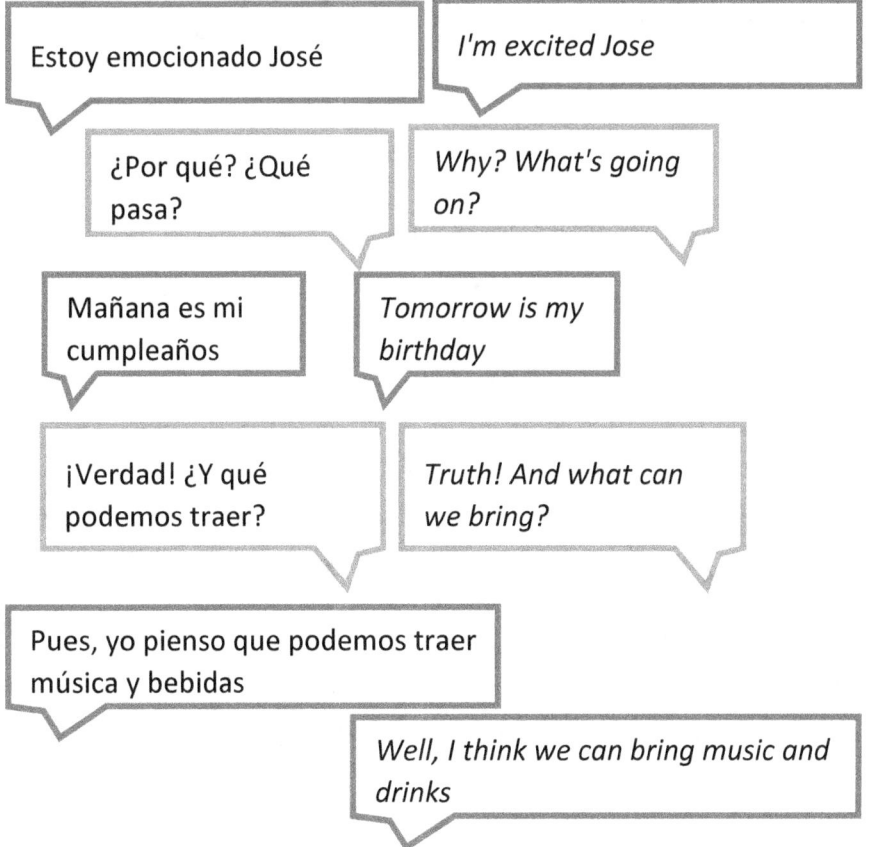

Buena idea. Yo puedo traer las cosas para hacer un karaoke	Good idea. I can bring the things to do karaoke
¡Ja ja ja ja! Suena bien	Ha ha ha! Sounds good
Y hoy hablo con María para ver si puede traer un pastel	And today I talk to Maria to see if she can bring a cake
¡Me encanta la idea!	I love the idea!

> 💡 The most important information to obtain from this conversation could be the fact that because they are both at the office and everything they are planning to get to the party, they are planning to bring it to the same place where they are talking, they won't move to a different point, or more precisely, they won't bring the things to a different place. And that's why the verb to use is "traer" which has the meaning of "bringing here"

Do I need to use "ir" or "venir" before "traer" or "llevar" to avoid confusion? The answer is no.

As you have might noticed, in Spanish the context is very important, and because of this, that's why the verbs need to be very specific, in meaning and also in conjugation. There's a lot of information that can be avoided or replaced just by using the right verb.

Let's say someone goes to the supermarket and will bring a soda from there. That person can explain everything without falling into a confusing situation, just by using the right verb.

For example: Yo voy al mercado y traigo una soda.

In the example, the person is explaining that he/she goes to the supermarket: **"voy al supermercado"** and also is explaining that will get back with a soda: **"traigo una soda"**

Everything is well explained and native speakers will only understand that this person goes and comes back with the soda.

Another example: Voy a la fiesta y traigo algo para ti.

Pay attetion! The person goes to the party: **"voy a la fiesta"** and he/she (will) return to the same place with something from the party, that's what the person explains by saying **"traigo algo para ti"**. He/she is not bringing something for you at the party, on the contrary, he/she will get with something from the party, for you.

Part VI: Verbal Periphrasis

> A verbal periphrasis is when in a sentence, a single action is built with two or more verbs. Actions like *"being able to do something"*, *"wanting to do something"* and the composition of the future tense *"going to do something"* are some examples of a verbal periphrasis. In Spanish, this structure can be applied and it will become helpful for you in the first steps on this language

In Spanish, this structure is very common, is basic and there are some useful verbs you can use to create verbal periphrasis.

In order to correctly apply this form, there is a important rule to learn and put in practice. Check these examples:

I can do sport / **"Yo puedo hacer deporte"**

I know (how to) speak Spanish / **"Yo sé (cómo) hablar español"**

I want to go to Cuba / **"Yo quiero ir a Cuba"**

I have to buy food / **"Yo tengo que comprar comida"**

Check how the verbs are conjugated, the first in the sentence is conjugated with its noun, but the next one remains in its infinite form. This is how verbal periphrasis are made in Spanish. **"First verb conjugated + second verb in infinite form"**

To add information to this topic here are the most common verbs you can put in practice to create verbal periphrasis:

		English	Spanish
Poder (can)		*I can learn Spanish*	**Yo puedo aprender Español**
Querer (to want)		*I want to travel*	**Yo quiero viajar**
Tener que (to have to)	+ A verb in infinitive form	*I have to practice*	**Yo tengo que practicar**
Saber (to know)		*I know (how to) swim*	**Yo sé (cómo) nadar**
Pensar (to think)		*I think (about) going to Mexico*	**Yo pienso (sobre) ir a México**
Ir a (to go to)		*I'm going to buy a phone*	**Yo voy a comprar un teléfono**

💡 The verbal periphrasis is a conjugated verb followed by a verb in infinitive form, in that list, the periphrasis made with the verbs "poder", "querer", "saber" are directly followed with a verb in infinitive form.

But on the contrary, there are other verbs that have slightly different structures for example:

"tener que" for example: I have to work / "**Yo tengo que trabajar**"

As you can see, the particle "que" goes in the middle of the conjugated verb and the infinite form of the other verb "tener **que** hacer" / *have to do.*

But in addition, there's the composition of the future tense *"going to"* which won't be added on this book, but it might be interesting for you to know/understand that this composition is possible in Spanish and it's formed with the verb and the preposition **"ir a"** and then a verb in infinitive form; for example: *"I'm going to buy a car"* / **"Yo voy a comprar un carro"**

To have some examples of these verbs, check these conversations:

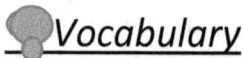Vocabulary

Within this vocabulary you will find practical verbs for daily life which will come handy when speaking Spanish. Remember always you can go to the end of the book to find these verbs and some others!

Verbs in English	*Translation Spanish*
To travel	"**viajar**"
To buy	"**comprar**"
To know (a place)	"**conocer**"
To live	"**vivir**"
To work	"**trabajar**"
To ask (a favor)	"**pedir**"

Conversation 1: Giving opinions

Context: Paola wants to visit some places; she talks to her friend Miguel about it.

> Miguel, quiero ir a México

> *Miguel, I want to go to Mexico.*

¡Qué bien!	Very nice!
Sí y quiero pedir recomendaciones	Yes and I want to ask for recommendations
¿Qué lugares puedo visitar?	What places can I visit?
Bueno mira, tienes que visitar Cancún y también las pirámides	Well look, you have to visit Cancun and also the pyramids
Ok, ¿y qué comida puedo comer?	Okay, and what food can I eat?
¡Ah sí! Tienes que probar los tamales y las carnitas	Oh, yes! You have to try the tamales and carnitas
¿Y hay alguna fiesta famosa?	And is there a famous party?

¡Sí! El día de los muertos, pero es en noviembre

Yes! The day of the dead, but it's in November

¡Falta poco!

Almost there!

Chapter 3:

Dates, Numbers and Time

On this chapter we'll explore how vocabulary related to time, numbers, and dates. Within these pages you will find how numbers work in Spanish, how to tell the time and also how to explain moments in specific dates and moments of the day too.

Content

- ➢ Moments of the day
- ➢ Days of the week
- ➢ Month of the year
- ➢ Numbers
- ➢ Prices
- ➢ Telling the time

Part I: Numbers

> Numbers will be the first part of this chapter, here you will learn how to translate them into Spanish and also how to use them when talking about prices and telling the time

Numbers

the composition of cardinal numbers in Spanish has no great difference from English. Two-cipher numbers work in the same way, i.e. *"Twenty-one"* where the tens are placed first and the units.

 Vocabulary

Within this vocabulary you will find numbers from 0 to *Thousands* and "a million" which will become practical during this chapter.

From 0 to 29	*From 30 to 91*	*From 100 to 2000*	*A million*
0. cero	30. Treinta	100. Cien	Un millón
1. Uno	31. Treinta y uno	101. Ciento uno	
2. Dos	32. Treinta y dos	102. Ciento dos	
3. Tres	28. Veintiocho	200. Doscientos	
4. Cuatro	29. Veintinueve	300. Trescientos	
5. Cinco	40. Cuarenta	400. Cuatrocientos	
6. Seis	41. Cuarenta y uno	500. Quinientos	
7. Siete	50. Cincuenta	600. Seiscientos	
8. Ocho	51. Cincuenta y uno	700. Setecientos	
9. Nueve	60. Sesenta	800. Ochocientos	
10. Diez	61. Sesenta y uno	900. Novecientos	
11. Once	70. Setenta	1000. Mil	
12. Doce	71. Setenta y uno	2000. Dos mil	
13. Trece	80. Ochenta		
14. Catorce	81. Ochenta y uno		
15. Quince	90. Noventa		
16. Dieciséis	91. Noventa y uno		
17. Diecisiete			
18. Dieciocho			

19. Diecinueve
20. Veinte
21. Veintiuno
22. Veintidós
23. Veintitrés
24. Veinticuatro
25. Veinticinco
26. Veintiséis
29. Veintinueve

The reason why they are separated into 3 rows is because of the way you have to write or count the numbers in Spanish. From 0 to 29 it's a single word, **1=uno**, **15=quince**, **24=veinticuatro.**

But then, from 31 to 99 the writing is divided. For example:

31= treina y uno *and not* treintiuno

54= cincuenta y cuatro *and not* cincuenticuatro

98 = noventa y ocho *and not* noventiocho

As a helpful tip, you might hear people saying *"noventicuatro"* as if it's a single word some others might even write that number in one word, but the reason is because of the fonetic link formed when speaking fast, thus "noven**ta y** cuatro" can fonetically become "noven**ti**cuatro" but writing the number like that, would be an error.

About hundreds, they are also divided into 2 (or three) quantities: "hundreds + tens and units" and no "and" comes between hundreds and tens like in English. For example:

126 = one hundred **and** twenty-six *becomes* "**ciento veintiseis**"

You can check in the list above that "100" has to forms: "cien" and "ciento".

"Cien" will be always used when you have a hundred without other numbers. So **100 will be always "cien"**.

But starting from "101", the word "cien" becomes "ciento" and it will be like that up to "199". For example:

102 = **"ciento dos"**

110 = **"ciento diez"**

195 = **"ciento noventa y cinco"** and "95" remains in two separated words **"noventa y cinco"** because this grammar rule will not change, no matter the situation.

The similar situation will happen with thousands. For example:

1001 = **"mil uno"**

1010 = **"mil diez"**

1100 = **"mil cien"**

1535 = **"mil quinientos treinta y cinco** in this last example you can observe that each quantity is separated and **"treinta y cinco"** keeps the same format.

To complete this idea, "two thousand" for example would be **"dos mil"**, "three thousand" = **"tres mil"**, "ten thousand" = **"diez mil"**…

Starting from "millions", "one million" = **"un millón"**, "two million" = **"dos millones"**, "ten million" = **"diez millones"**…

In addition to these facts, there's something quite interesting in Spanish, **numbers have gender** when they work as adjectives. And this is how it works:

- **Numbers as adjectives**: in Spanish, even numbers need to follow the rules when they are working as adjectives. For example: *"hundreds of people"* will have to be translated as **"cientos de personas"** in which **"cientos"** is plural because it has to match with **"personas"** which is plural too.

  But this doesn't happen with every number, just a few of them. Here is the list of those who need to change:

  - **One:** when the situation needs it, the number "one" can or have to change into two additional forms. For example:

    "one house" *becomes* "**una** casa"
    "one cup of coffee" *becomes* "**una** taza"

    This is when the noun is feminine. When it's masculine, *"one"* becomes **"un"** like the indefinite article. Observe these examples:

    "one friend" / "**un amigo**"
    "one man" / "**un hombre**"
    "one country" / "**un país**"

  - **Hundreds:** Also, hundreds, starting from "200" have to match gender and not quantity because it will remain always plural. To complete the idea, it will start only from 200 and on because situations with "one hundred" will be always "masculine" or neutral. It doesn't have to change into some feminine form. Check these examples:

    "two hundred people" / "**doscientas personas**"

"seven hundred and seventy-five tons / **"setecientas setenta y cinco toneladas"**

These for feminine words. For masculine words, the number remains the same "doscientos", "trescientos", "quinientos". For example:

"five hundred boys" / **"quinientos niños"**

"three hundred meters / **"trescientos metros"**

o **Thousands and millions:** As a final point, thousands and millions work in a slightly different way.

For thousands it only matches when it appears with no other quantity. Example: "thousands of people" / **"miles de personas".**

When it's composed of a bigger quantity, only the hundreds will match, but the word "thousand" will remain the same. For example:

"two thousand people" / **"dos mil personas"**

"five hundred and fifty thousand things" / **"quinientas cincuenta mil cosas"** in this specific example you can learn that only **"quinientas"** is matching with the feminine noun **"cosas".**

"Millions" will only have two forms, when it's only *"one million"* which in Spanish would be **"un millón"** and starting from *"two million"* and on, in which it would change into its plural form **"millones"**. And they won't match with the noun's gender. I.e. "Million people" / **"millones de personas".**

> **Pricing:** in this specific point, you will learn how to talk about prices, how to ask for it, and how to answer.

All of the worldwide currencies are "male", which means that all of the prices will be said as if they are "male nouns". The only common exception we find in Spanish is with India's currency which is *"the rupee"* / **"la rupia"** and *"pounds"* / **"libras"** and these specific cases will require a "female" quantity.

Euros, dollars, yens, pounds… they are all male nouns. Check this list to add more information about this vocabulary: *Remember you can always check this and other vocabularies in the section "vocabulary" in the last pages of this book.

Common vocabulary about money:

Names in English	Translation Spanish
Euro/Euros	"euro/euros" (masc.)
Dollar/Dollars	"dólar/dólares" (masc.)
Pound/Pounds	"libra/libras" (fem.)
Yen/Yens	"yen/yenes" (masc.)
Coin	"moneda" (fem.)
Currency	"moneda" (fem.)
Money	"Dinero" (masc.) or "plata" (fem.)
Cash	"Efectivo" (masc.)
Cost / price	"Costo"/"precio"
To pay	"Pagar"
To charge	"Cobrar"
To save (money)	"ahorrar"
To spend	"gastar"
Cheap	"Barato(a)"
Expensive	"Caro(a)"

Conversation 1: At the restaurant

Context: Carlos is ordering some food at the restaurant, he's asking for prices

Conversation 2: Calling to book on a hotel

Context: Ana calls to the hotel "vista bonita" to ask for prices

| ¡Hola! ¿Es el hotel vista bonita? | Hello! Is the hotel a beautiful view? |

| Sí, buenas tardes, ¿en qué puedo ayudarte? | Yes, good afternoon, can I help you? |

| Quiero saber cuál es el precio de la habitación por noche | I want to know what the price of the room per night is |

| Tenemos varios precios: Una habitación sencilla cuesta 50 La habitación doble cuesta 70 y la Premium cuesta 120 | We have several prices: A single room costs 50 The double room costs 70 and the Premium costs 120 |

> *Good choice. I also tell you that the price includes breakfast and dinner in the restaurant*

Me interesa la habitación doble.

> *I'm interested in the double room.*

Buena elección. También le digo que el precio incluye desayuno y cena en el restaurante

Genial. Quiero reservar 5 días

> *That's great. I want to book 5 days*

Conversation 3: At the mall

Context: José wants to buy a laptop; he wants a good price but also good quality

In this next part, let's focus on ordinal numbers. Ordinal numbers are those who stablish order to ideas, people, facts...

In English they are known as *"first", "second", "third"* ... and they also exist in Spanish for the same purpose, stablishing order. The only difference is that, because usually they are used as adjectives or adverbs, they have will have different translation to match gender and quantity.

The idea of this content is to bring you all the practical information you would need or hear in daily life.

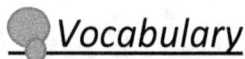*Vocabulary*

Within this vocabulary you will find words related to ordinal numbers from 1st to 100th.

From 1st to 10th	*From 11th to 19th*	*From 100th to 1000th*
1er. primer(o)/(a)	11vo. decimoprimer(o)/(a)	100mo centésimo(a)
2do. segundo(a)	12vo. decimosegundo(a)	1000mo milésimo(a)
3ero. tercero(a)	13vo. Decimotercero(a)	
4to. cuarto(a)	14vo. Decimocuarto(a)	
5to. quinto(a)	15vo. Decimoquinto(a)	
6to. sexto(a)	16vo. decimosexto(a)	
7mo. séptimo(a)	17vo. decimoséptimo(a)	
8vo. octavo(a)	18vo. Decimoctavo(a)	
9no. novena(a)	19vo. Decimonoveno(a)	
10mo. décimo(a)	20mo vigésimo(a)	
	21ero vigésimo primer(o)/(a)	
	22do vigésimo segundo(a)	
	.	
	29no (vigésimo noveno)	
	30mo trigésimo(a)	
	40mo cuadragésimo(a)	
	50mo quincuagésimo(a)	
	60mo sexagésimo(a)	
	70mo septuagésimo(a)	
	80mo octagésimo(a)	
	90mo nonagésimo(a)	

> 💡 As you can observe, every number has masculine and feminine form, they also have plural form when the situation requires it.
>
> As a practical fact, even though ordinal numbers exist and they have their own word/vocabulary, sometimes it is correct to just name the number if it was a "cardinal". For example:
>
> - *This is the fiftieth anniversary/* **Este es el quincuagésimo aniversario**
> - *This is the fiftieth anniversary/* **Este es el cincuenta aniversario**
>
> As you can observe, the two translations are valid. But this is only commonly possible with higher numbers. For *"first", "second", "third"* it is better to use the ordinal form. And native people also prefer to use this form as well.

An effective practice is always good, check these texts to find common ways you can put ordinal numbers in practice:

Text 1: Sending an itinerary

Context: Alejandro runs a tour company; he sends a message to his client to explain the itinerary for the first day of his trip in Colombia

De: Agencia Latin Adventure

Para: mt24@-email.com

Buenos días,

Envío en este mensaje el itinerario de la ruta para su viaje a Colombia.

Ustedes tienen el primer vuelo. A las 6:00am. Llegan a Colombia a las 12pm.

En el aeropuerto espera un taxi para el hotel.

El hotel "Dorado" es el segundo mejor hotel de Colombia

La primera actividad es las 3pm. Es una visita al museo de arte moderno.

La segunda actividad, a las 5pm es a la zona turística "el poblado".

La tercera y última actividad del día es una fiesta en el hotel, desde las 10 hasta las 4am.

Translation 1:

From: Latin Adventure Agency

To: mt24@-email.com

Good Morning,

I send in this message the route itinerary for your trip to Colombia.

You guys have the first flight. At 6:00 am. They arrive in Colombia at 12pm.

A taxi is waiting at the airport for the hotel.

The "Dorado" hotel is the second-best hotel in Colombia

The first activity is 3pm. It is a visit to the museum of modern art.

The second activity, at 5pm is to the tourist area "the town".

The third and last activity of the day is a party at the hotel, from 10am to 4am

Conversation 2: Results from a contest

Context: The announcer tells the people the results of the contest

¡Damas y caballeros!	*Ladies and gentlemen!*
Finalmente tenemos los ganadores de la vigésima primera competencia de tenis:	*Finally, we have the winners of the twenty-first tennis competition:*
En primer lugar: Alejandro Castillo	*First: Alejandro Castillo*
Segundo lugar para: Juan González	*Second place for: Juan González*
Tercer lugar: José Londoño	*Third place: José Londoño*
Todos son ganadores y nosotros estamos muy felices por los resultados.	*They are all winners and we are very happy with the results.*

Conversation 3: At work

Context: Mr. Danilo M is talking to his sale manager Juan; he explains the goals for this month in the company

> Juan tenemos que aumentar las ventas. ¿Qué podemos hacer?

Juan, we have to increase sales. What can we do?

> Jefe, primero necesitamos cambiar nuestra campaña publicitaria

Boss, first we need to change our ad campaign

> Tienes mi ayuda y el presupuesto. ¿Qué más necesitas?

You have my help and the budget. What else do you need?

> Segundo, necesitamos cambiar a dos de nuestro equipo

Second, we need to change two of our team

> Si las razones son justas, podemos hacerlo

If the reasons are fair, we can do it

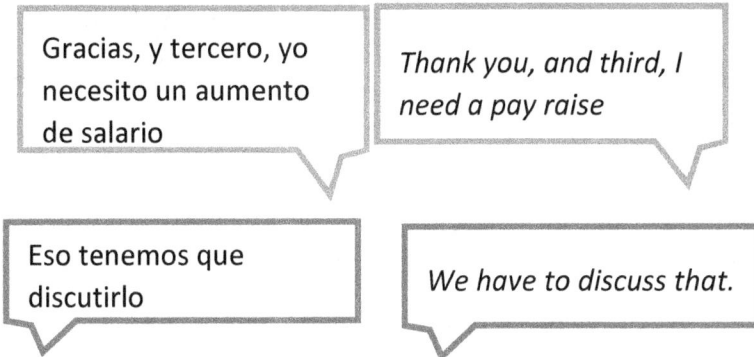

Part II: Telling the time

In Spanish, telling the time has multiple ways to do it. There are translations even for expressions such as "o'clock", "and a half" ...

Words like *"a.m"* or *"p.m"* also exist in Spanish and they can be used to make reference to "morning" or "noon/afternoon/night"

- **How to tell the time**: in Spanish, the same way as in English, the 12-hour system is used, they are divided into hours a.m. and p.m.

  To ask for the time, the question in Spanish is "¿qué hora es?" and a common variation **"¿qué hora tienes?"** and even **"¿qué horas son?"** but the most common and international is the first one.

To answer, the time is introduced by "**son las**" and it has to be plural because in Spanish, it is understood as plural. For example:

"6:00" = "**son las seis**"

"8:00" = "**son las ocho**"

"11:00" = "**son las once**"

There's only one exception as is a common mistake made by even native people, when talking about 1:00 and on, the time has to be said in "singular form" of "ser". Observe these examples:

"1:00" = "**es la una**"

"1:53 = "**es la una cincuenta y tres**"

Even the article has to be in singular form.

💡 Don't get surprised if you hear someone saying "**son las 1**" because that's one of the most common mistakes and people don't pay attention to it. Although, it is a grammatical error.

Telling the time has different ways of creating the sentence. You can name number after number, separate hours and minutes with the conjunction "y" or if the situation allows it, you can explain how many minutes are left for the next hour. Also "a quarter", "a half" and "o`clock" have their own translations in Spanish. Check the list below:

- "**O'clock**" = the translation for this expression is "**en punto**". For example:

    It's nine o'clock / "**Son las nueve en punto**"

    It's ten o'clock / "**Son las diez en punto**"

- "**A quarter**" = "**(un) cuarto**" is used either for 15 minutes past an hour, or 15 minutes to the next hour:

    "It's a quarter past four" / "**Son las cuatro y cuarto**"

    "It's a quarter to five" / "**Son un cuarto para las cinco**"

- "**A half**" = "**y media**". Check these examples to understand its use:

    "It's a half past five" / "**Son las cinco y media**"

    "It's seven and a half" / "**Son las siete y media**"

All of these expresions can be used, but also, telling hour + minutes works exactly the same and it just depend on the speaker, there's no formal or informal way to tell the time in Spanish. Sometimes news for example, might prefer to tell the time without using these expressions.

Here are the ways you can tell the time when it's not one of the cases above:

"5:38" = "**las cinco y treinta y ocho**" or "**las cinco treinta y ocho**"

"12:24" = "**las doce y veinticuatro**" or "**las doce veinticuatro**"

"6:30" = "**las seis y treinta**", "**las seis treinta**" or "**las seis y media**"

"7:45" = **"las siete (y) cuarenta y cinco"** or **"un cuarto para las siete"**

"8:15" = **"las ocho (y) quince"** or **"las ocho y cuarto"**

And there are additional situations in which the speaker might prefer to explain the few minutes left for the next hour, in situations like "5:57", "4:48" or "3:50". In these examples, the sentences could be as follows:

"5:57" = **"faltan tres para las seis"**

"4:48" = **"faltan doce para las cinco"**

"3:50" = **"faltan diez para las cuatro"**

In which the use of "falta" is needed. "Falta" is a defective verb used to explain *"what's left"*. Thus, in the first case, **"faltan tres para las seis"** could be translated as "three minutes left to six".

 Feel free to use any of those ways, no matter the

Part II: The date

In this part of the chapter, you will learn how to tell the date, using the common structure, learning new vocabulary (days and months) and putting in practice the numbers and interrogative particles.

To start this part, here's the vocabulary for days of the week and months of the year. All of them are masculine nouns.

Days of the week	*"Días de la semana"*
Monday	lunes
Tuesday	martes
Wednesday	miércoles
Thursday	jueves
Friday	viernes
Saturday	sábado
Sunday	domingo
Weekend	fin de semana

Months of the year	*"Meses del año"*
January	enero
February	febrero
March	marzo
April	abril
May	mayo
June	Junio
July	Julio
August	Agosto
September	Septiembre
October	Octubre
November	Noviembre
December	Diciembre

➢ **How to tell the date**: in Spanish, the common format is DD/NN/MM/YY. Following this idea check these examples:

What's your date of birth? / **¿Cuál es tu fecha de nacimiento?**

It's October 14th, 1993 / **"Es el 14 de octubre de 1993"**

When is your birhday? / **¿Cuándo es tu cumpleaños?**

February 26th / **"El 26 de febrero"**

💡 You can observe the translations for each situation and also the inexistence of ordinal format for the date's number. **If you want to check the vocabulary about ordinal numbers, give it a look to the "vocabulary section" at the end of the book**

Chapter 4:

Possessives

On this chapter, you will learn about possessives adjectives, how to use the genitive "'s" and also this book will show you a practical vocabulary related to family.

Content

- Possessive adjectives
- The use of genitive "'s" in Spanish
- Family members

Part I: Possessive adjectives

> In Spanish, nouns and adjectives will have gender, talking about possessive adjectives (my, your, his, her…) will have translations that have to match with the noun's gender.

Possessives in Spanish work matching the gender and quantity of the *"thing"* the noun possesses and not the gender and quantity of the noun itself.

Before moving forward with the examples and explanation, here is the vocabulary of possessive adjectives:

Personal Pronoun	**Adjectivos posesivos**	**Translation English**
Yo	**mi/mis**	my
Tú	**tu/tus**	your
Él/Ella	**su/sus**	his/her
Nosotros/Nosotras	**nuestro(s) nuestra(s)**	our
Usted	**su/sus**	your
Ustedes	**su/sus**	your
Ellos / Ellas	**su/sus**	their

 From that vocabulary we can clarify some critical points:

- The differences between the two choices of each possessive in Spanish is related to quantity (singular and plural).
- "Our" has 4 translations in Spanish, two of the are singular (masculine and feminine form) and the other 2 are their plural forms; *"nuestro"*, *"nuestra"*, *"nuestros"*, *"nuestras"*
- **"His/her" have only one translation "su"** and its plural form **"sus"**
- The possessive "su/sus" belongs to the rest of the pronouns, and remember they do not match with the noun, but with the object that it is possessing.

> **How possessive adjectives work in Spanish:** every possessive has to match in quantity (and in gender if you are using "our") with the object. Check these examples to start learning about the way they work:

"My house is in México" / **"Mi casa está en México"**
"My friends are here!" / **"¡Mis amigos están aquí!"** = **"¡Mis amigas están aquí"**
"Your family lives in Honduras?" / **"¿Tu familia vive en Honduras?"**
"Your things are at home" / **"Tus cosas están en casa"**

These pronouns match with quantity only as you can observe. But on the contrary, the translation for the possessive *"our"* has to match with gender and quantity. Check these examples:

"Our country is beautiful" / **"Nuestro país es hermoso"**
"Our house is blue" / **"Nuestra casa es azul"**
"Our friends are Mexican" / **"Nuestros amigos son mexicanos"**
"Our daughters are at school" / **"Nuestras hijas están en la escuela"**

This situation is different, "our" is the only possessive that has 4 different translations in Spanish.

In addition, "su" and "sus" require practice because they can make reference to multiple pronouns. In Spanish, the noun can be omitted and this will produce conversations in which "él/ella/usted/ustedes/ellos…" won't appear and might difficult the comprehension of the idea. Sometimes even for native speakers might be necessary the use of pronouns to explain who's possessing something. Observe these examples:

"Sir, do you need your hat?" / **"Señor, ¿necesita (usted) su sombrero?"**

"She lives in an appartment with her dog" / **"(Ella) vive en un apartamento con su perro"**

"I want to talk with their parents" / **"(Yo) quiero hablar con sus padres"** (The parents of the students for example)

"I am with your friends / **"(Yo) estoy con sus amigos"**

Check how the same adjective is used for different pronouns. Also observe that they are not matching the pronoun (sir, ella, yo…).

Now, take time to read these conversations:

 Vocabulary

Before the conversations, take a look at this vocabulary, it's related to family and will help you expand your knowledge in Spanish:

Family Members	*"Miembros de la familia"*
Grandfather	**Abuelo**
Grandmother	**Abuela**
Mother/Mom	**Madre/Mamá**
Father/Dad	**Padre/Papá**
Son/Daughter	**Hijo/Hija**
Brother/Sister	**Hermano/Hermana**
Siblings	**Hermanos**
Uncle/Aunt	**Tío/Tía**
Cousin	**Primo/Prima**
Nephew	**Sobrino/Sobrina**

Text 1: Family

Context: Gabriela has a presentation at school, she needs to talk about her family

Hola, hoy vengo a hablar de mi familia.

Mi mamá se llama Juana y tiene 48, mi papá es Andrés y tiene 48 tambien.

En casa somos 2 hermanos y yo. Mi hermano mayor se llama Carlos y mi hermano menor es un bebé, tiene 9 meses.

Mis abuelos viven en otra ciudad, se llaman Carmen y Sergio. Mi abuela tiene 80 y mi abuelo 83. Ellos viven con su perrito y un gato que se llama manchas.

También tengo tíos. Mi tía Alejandra tiene 34 y mi tío Alberto tiene 40.

Tengo solo 1 primo, José. Ellos todos viven aquí en Chile.

Translation 1:

Hello, today I come to talk about my family.

My mom is Juana and she is 48, my dad is Andrés and he is 48 too.

At home there are 2 brothers and me. My older brother is called Carlos and my younger brother is a baby, he is 9 months old.

My grandparents live in another city, their names are Carmen and Sergio. My grandmother is 80 and my grandfather 83. They live with their puppy and a cat called spots.

I also have uncles. My aunt Alejandra is 34 and my uncle Alberto is 40.

I have only 1 cousin, José. They all live here in Chile.

My family is important and I love everyone very much.

Part II: Genitive "'s" in Spanish

> The structure of the saxon genitive allows the English speaker to reduce or replace parts of the sentences into shorter structures. But this tool doesn't exist in Spanish, thus, the sentences will always have a longer version compared to English.

Sentences in which in which the genitive explains who's possessing an object will have a longer translation. For example: *"María's car"* will be literally translated as *"The car of María"*. Or *"Daniel's cellphone" / "The cellphone of Daniel"*. This due to the inexistence in Spanish, of a structure that can directly replace the saxon genitive in English.

Here's a small activity for you to practice and improve the understanding of this point:

Exercise: translate the following sentences into Spanish. Remember there is no structure for genitive and the sentences have to be translated "word-by-word"

    a. *The boy's apple*

    _____

    b. *María's house*

    _____

    c. *My mom's house*

    _____

d. *Your friend's dog*

_____

e. *Our country's map* ("mapa")

_____

> 💡 These "longer structures" also happen with sentences such as: *"Spanish lesson", "Gold watch", "Weekend", "Independence Day", "Math teacher"* all of these structures don't work the same way in Spanish, they need a longer form:
>
> - *"Spanish lesson"* / **"Lecciones de español"**
> - *"Gold watch"* / **"Reloj de oro"**
> - *"Weekend"* / **"Fin de semana"**
> - *"Independence Day"* / **"Día de la independencia"**
> - *"Math teacher"* / **"Maestro de matemáticas"**
>
> As you can compare, the structures work literally *"The lessons of Spanish", "The watch of gold", "The end of the week"*…

Chapter 5:

Sentence Complements

The spoken chain is linear because it is made up of linguistic signs that are mutually supportive, one appears and another succeeds it in a coordinated way. In Spanish, contrary to English, as we said before, the constituents of a statement or sentence have a fairly flexible order of appearance, the subject may appear at the beginning, at the center or at the end, however the statement is grammatically valid. The same can happen with the verb locations or the verbal complements which admit diverse displacements simply with the intention of marking a certain communicational emphasis.

In this chapter, you will learn how components can be added to a sentence in Spanish and how verbs can interact with them.

Content

- ➢ Direct Object Complements
- ➢ Indirect Object Complements
- ➢ Object Pronouns
- ➢ Circumstantial Complements
- ➢ Position of Object Pronouns in Different Verb Structures

In general, complements are the parts of the sentence that serve to complete the meaning of the verb, to provide more information.

For example, we can observe how the following sentence is succeeded by others with displacement of the original constituents of the first: the meaning is not altered in any case but its emphasis is placed in a different position.

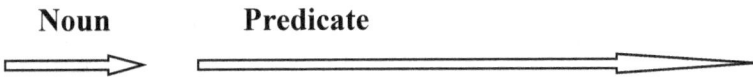

*Juliana **tuvo** muchas reuniones en el trabajo* / *Juliana had a lot of meetings at work*

NS   NV   DC or DO   CC

Where:

> ➤ "**NS**" is the "noun" or "Nominal Subject"
> ➤ "**NV**" is the "verb" or "Nominal Verb"
> ➤ "**DC/DO**" is the "Direct Complement or Direct Object"
> ➤ "**CC**" is the "Circumstantial Complement"

In this sentence the emphasis is on the subject:

What did Juliana have? Many meetings.

Where did she have them? At work.

The two complements require the action of the verb "tener".

*Muchas reuniones **tuvo** Juliana en el trabajo.*

In this sentence the change of emphasis is on the event.

*Juliana en el trabajo **tuvo** muchas reuniones.*

And in this last sentence, the emphasis is on the place.

As you can see, in Spanish, the parts of this chain can be alternated without affecting the meaning of the sentence. This structure allows the speaker to switch the order of the components always following the succession of parts without losing the logical meaning or sense.

Part I: Direct Complement or Direct Object

> The function of the Direct Complement, also called the Direct Object, is to specify the meaning of the transitive verb. That is, if the OD is not present, the meaning of the verb is not clear to us.

For example:

Juliana had... It is evident that in order to understand the statement we would require more information.

The sofa was... It does not communicate because it is an unfinished sentence, it is ungrammatical. If we completed it with: **in the living room**, it would be intelligible and grammatically valid.

It can be also explained as the "flask" or "recipient" of the action of a transitive verb. It is called "Object" because an object is something you can apply an action on.

In a sentence like "He took the keys". "The keys" become the direct object because is being completely affected by the action he did.

Another good example would be: "Peter hit him". In this case "him" is the direct object because this person becomes the receiver of the action.

How to recognize a Direct Object in Spanish:

When a transitive verb is in a sentence, a complement must be present in order to give the full meaning or result of the verb.

Check this sentence:

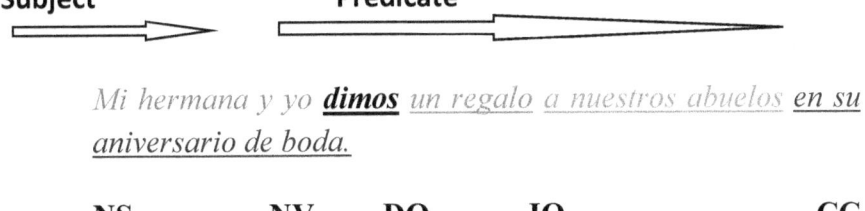

      NS   **NV**   **DO**   **IO**   **CC**

My sister and I gave a gift to our grandparents for their wedding anniversary

To recognize the DO in the sentence we can ask ourselves two questions:

    a) ¿What did we do? "We gave"
    b) ¿What did we give? "A gift"

In this case, "a gift" becomes the direct object because in Spanish is the recipient of the verb's action (to give).

Also, you can verify that the word is in fact a direct object when you can replace it with an object pronoun like "it" in a sentence like "I gave **the gift**" = "I gave **it**".

In Spanish the object pronouns are unique or different that in English and to know the differences will make your way easier when practicing this topic.

Direct Objects in Spanish:

Personal Pronoun	**Direct Object Pronoun**	
Yo	**me**	
Tú	**te**	
Él / Ella	**lo/la**	It differs on gender
Nosotros / Nosotras	**nos**	
Usted	**lo/la**	It differs on gender
Ustedes	**los/las**	
Ellos/Ellas	**los/las**	

Here you can find some new words "lo/la" and their plural forms "los/las". They can replace a person the same way you can say in English *"I saw **Tom**"* = *"I saw **him**"* or *"You helped **Maria and I**"* = *"You helped **us**"*

But they can also replace things, and it will depend on If it's singular or plural, masculine or feminine, in order to use the right direct object pronoun.

For example:

    I take **the cellphone** = I took **it** / "Yo tomo **el teléfono**" = "Yo **lo** tomo"

    I see **Maria** = I see **her** / "Yo veo **a María**" = "Yo **la** veo"

    I call **my friends** = I call **them** / "Yo llamo **a mis amigos**" = "Yo **los** llamo"

> I help **Anna and Judy** = I help **them** / "Yo ayudo **a Anna y a Judy**" = "Yo **las** ayudo"

In case you are referring to someone you don't know or the situation requires the use of formal pronoun "usted". You have to pay attention to the person's gender when replacing the noun for an object pronoun.

For example:

> Can I help **you Mr. Rodriguez?** = Can I help **you?** / "¿**Lo** puedo ayudar (Sr. Rodriguez)?"

> Can I help **you Mrs. Rodriguez?** = Can I help **you?** / "¿**La** puedo ayudar (Sra. Rodriguez)?"

Here are two interesting situations compared to English, the object pronoun "**lo/la**" would be necessary and the sentence can't be correctly written or said if the object pronoun is missing when talking about the formal situation in which you have to use "Usted".

This structure "Yo ayudo **a usted**" as a translation for "I help **you (sir/lady)**" is incorrect in Spanish.

It has to be "Yo **lo/la** ayudo a usted".

Try not to get confused by these examples or specific situations, the further you go on this book and the more you practice and improve your skills, the more you will understand this easier and better.

Think about the first time you had to count apples and write the quantity as a number in the preschool. It was very hard. But then you keep growing up, practicing and that complex situation became very simple with time. That's all part of the learning process!

Part II: Indirect Complement or Indirect Object

> The Indirect Complement (IC) also called Indirect Object (IO) makes reference to the person or thing that receives the result of a verbal action. The OI will be always preceded by a preposition and it needs -in common situations- the existence of an Indirect Object Pronoun (IOP) to let the listener or reader know that the verb's result will affect someone or something indirectly.

Observe this sentence:

Noun   **Predicate**

⇨

(Nosotros) le **_escribimos_** un e-mail **_a la chica ganadora del concurso_**.

NS   **IOP**   **NV**   **DO**   **IO**

We write a mail to the winner of the contest

Sujeto   **Predicado**

⇨

Yo **_preparo_** *paella* **_para todos los presentes_**.

NS   **NV**   **DO**   **IO**

I prepare paella for the invited people

To identify or recognize the IO in a sentence, we can ask ourselves two questions:

    a) To who is the person doing the action?

    b) For who am I doing the action?

In this example, the sentence will be written twice, one would be a simple (but slightly incorrect) sentence, and the second one will be the full, totally correct sentence with a IOP.

Observe:

Por ejemplo:

Subject   **Predicate**

<u>Nosotros</u> **hablamos** *a los niños cada mañana.*
 NS   **NV**   **IO**   **CC**

We talk to the kids every morning

This sentence is understandable and it can be used as a direct translation from English to Spanish, but it isn't 100% correct. The IOP is missing and it should be included in the sentence to introduce the idea of who is being affected by the result of the verb.

Observe the sentence properly written in Spanish:

Subject   **Predicate**

<u>Nosotros</u> les **hablamos** *a los niños cada mañana.*
 NS   **IOP**   **NV**   **IO**   **CC**

Now the sentence doesn't sound weird in Spanish and it's because the IOP is included before the verb to let the person know that this action is affecting someone or something indirectly.

This is the way the sentences are fully built in Spanish, when object pronouns must be included.

The Indirect Object Pronouns are basically the same than the Direct Object Pronouns, but there's a different word that will be explained further and also compared to the previous pronouns.

Indirect Objects in Spanish:

Personal Pronoun	**Direct Object Pronoun**
Yo	**me**
Tú	**te**
Él / Ella	**le**
Nosotros / Nosotras	**nos**
Usted	**le**
Ustedes	**les**
Ellos/Ellas	**les**

When talking about IOP we don't find differences between genders when making references to "he/she/you…" this is because the indirect object doesn't completely replace a noun. Thus it's neutral and It can be seen as an additive to the sentence to give more sense to the action and what happens with it in the structure.

Check these examples in Spanish to better understand this idea:

*Damos libros **al niño*** ⟶ ***le** damos libros.*

*Damos libros **a los niños*** ⟶ ***les** damos libros.*

*Damos libros **a la niña*** ⟶ ***le** damos libros.*

*Damos libros **a las niñas*** ⟶ ***les** damos libros.*

In English, the sentences are translated as *"We give books to the boy/girl"* and *"We give books to the boys/girls"* and the detail you can observe is that the IOP is the same in all of the cases, and it only changes into its plural form when the action's result goes to a plural noun (the boys/the girls).

On the other hand, when we had this example: *"He takes **the cellphone** = He takes **it***" we replaced the "it" in Spanish with a direct object pronoun, because the action is completely affecting "the phone".

"Él toma **el teléfono**" = "Él **lo** toma"…

And we used the masculine form **"lo"** because *"cellphone"* is Spanish is a masculine noun and it's totally replaced by Direct Object Pronoun.

IOP vs DOP:

It is completely useless to try to understand verbs in Spanish the same way they work in English when talking about object pronouns. A verb can completely affect someone or something like for example *"hit him"* or it can just explain that it affects partially or indirectly like *"tell him"*. But verbs can exist along with direct or indirect objects depending on how the action is explained or wants to be explained in the sentence. For example, in Spanish, the sentence won't be the same if you take a slice from a pizza or if you take the whole pizza, the object pronoun will change.

Another good example is: if you say something to someone, it will use an indirect object pronoun.

If you say something without explaining who you told that to, i.e. "Say it!" this sentence will use a direct object pronoun.

Let's check the differences with these conversations:

Conversation 1: casual conversation

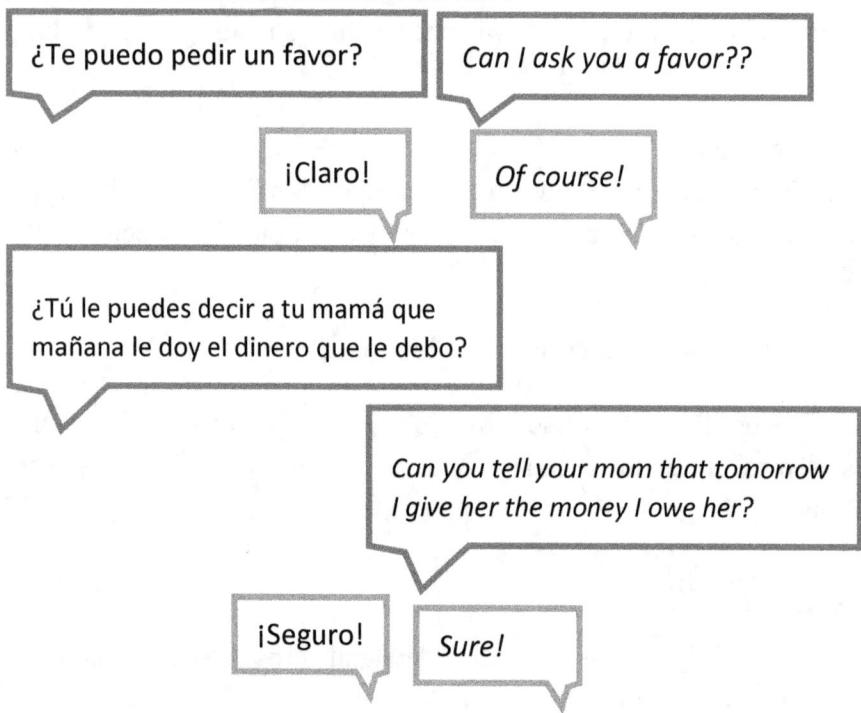

There are a couple of facts you can observe in this situation:

- "To tell"/"Decir" is followed by a preposition "a" which is telling you that it needs a IOP "le" to complete the sentence "**le** puedes **decir a**…"

- "To give"/"Dar" is also working with a preposition "give to" / "dar a" thus, it needs an indirect pronoun to explain that *"is the money I give **to** your mom"*

- "To owe"/"Deber" needs IOP for the same reason: *"the money I owe **to** your mom"*

Conversation 2: Casual conversation

Context: Two friends (Carlos and Juan) are about to say something important to Pedro:

This situation is different. Here are the observations:

- In this case, it's not about telling someone something, it's about saying something and, in this case, in Spanish, the verb has to be complemented with an Object Pronoun who will replace the "idea" or the "thing" the person will say.

Conversation 3: at home

Context: María offers Alejandro a pizza, but he's not hungry and will only take a slice.

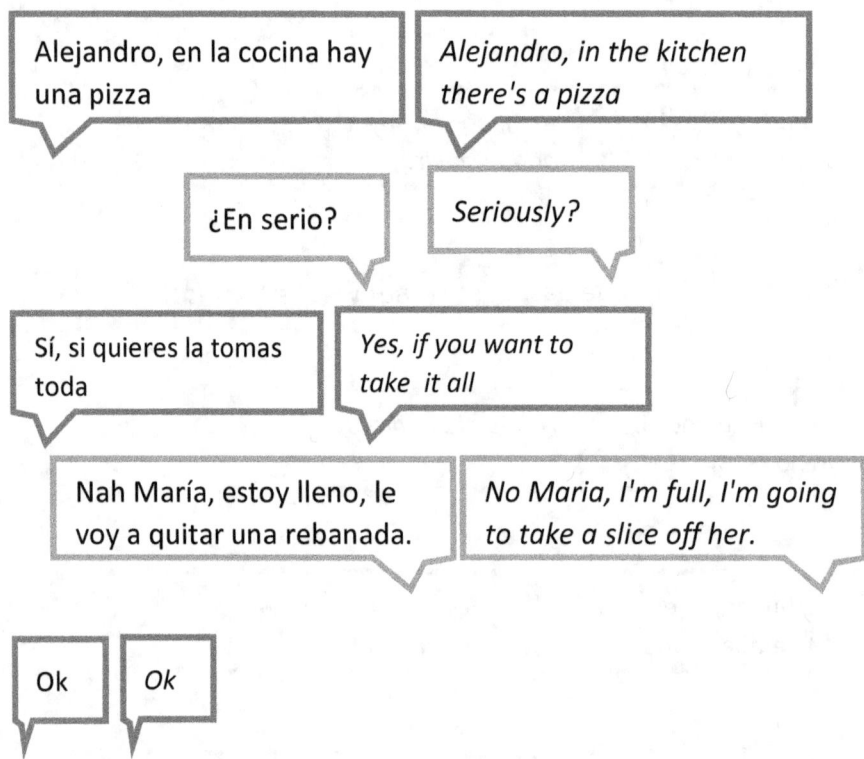

This conversation is different because you can observe indirect and direct pronouns. But why?

- In the first part, María says "take **it** all…" and in Spanish is translated as "**La** tomas toda". This is because María uses a pronoun to replace "the pizza" which in Spanish is a feminine word.
- But then Alejandro follows the conversation by saying that he's going to take only a slice (of the pizza) and in Spanish is translated as "**Le** voy a quitar". The "**le**" is the indirect object pronoun that explains the idea about not taking all the pizza, but just a single slice of it. **This is the difference about an action completely affecting a noun or just indirectly or incompletely affecting it.**

Conversation 4: Planning a birthday party

Context: María and Ana are planning what can they give to Andrés as a present for his birthday

Ana, mañana es el cumpleaños de Andrés	Ana, tomorrow is Tomorrow's Andrew's birthday.
¡Ah sí! ¿Le llevamos un regalo?	Ah, yes! Can we get you a present?
Sí, pienso que le podemos llevar una camisa. A él le encantan	Yes, I think we can bring him a shirt. He loves them

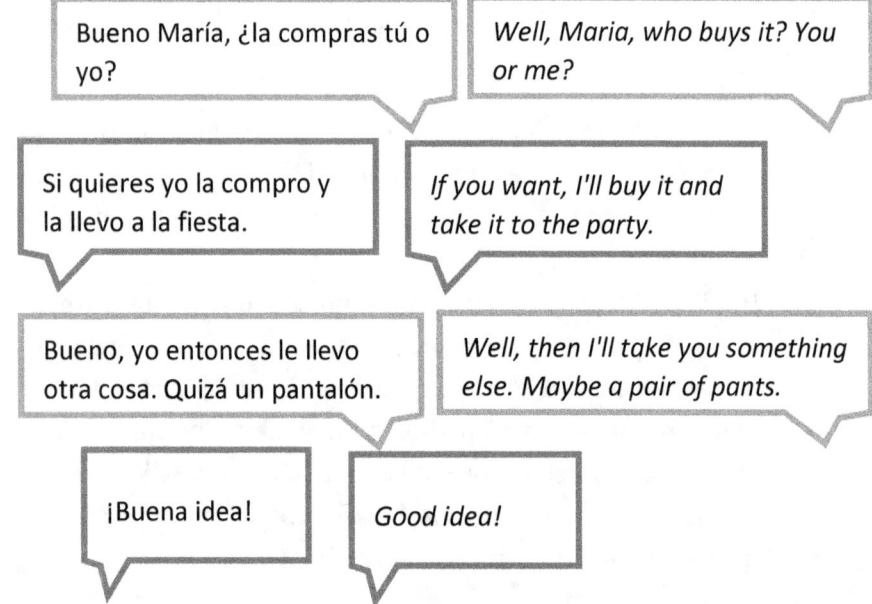

This last example works with different verbs. Here "bring" and "buy" go together with direct or indirect pronouns. Let's examine:

- In the first part María says *"Do we bring him a gift?"* and in Spanish is translated as "¿**Le** llevamos un regalo?". The **"le"** exists in the sentences because they are going to "bring something to him" thus, it requires an IOP in Spanish.
- Then Ana, in Spanish, proceeds with "**Le** llevamos una camisa" and the reason why the IOP is there, it's because they will "bring a shirt **to him**".
- About "to buy" it goes with either the IOP or DOP because of the situation. If it's *"buy it"* or if it's *"Buy the shirt **to him**"*

> 💡 On the other hand, the situations that require practice when talking about object complements are only when third persons are involved (he/she/it/they) and "usted/ustedes" in Spanish. For those cases you have to practice and learn how to correctly use "lo/la" or "le" -and their plural forms- depending on the action that is taking place. I.e.: *"take it", "say it", "tell him", "take him to a place", "take this to him"* ...
>
> If the first or second persons are involved, they will use the same word for direct or indirect objects, disregarding if the verb is affecting a noun totally or partially.
>
> Don't give up!

Part III: Circumstantial Complement

> The Circumstantial Complement (CC) provides more information about the action of the verb as it describes it, circumscribes in terms of: time, place, company, cause, instrument, mode, direction. So, there are several types of circumstantial Complements. This last point about the complements will give you a wider idea about how Spanish can work

Observe the following sentence, see how many Circumstantial Complements it has:

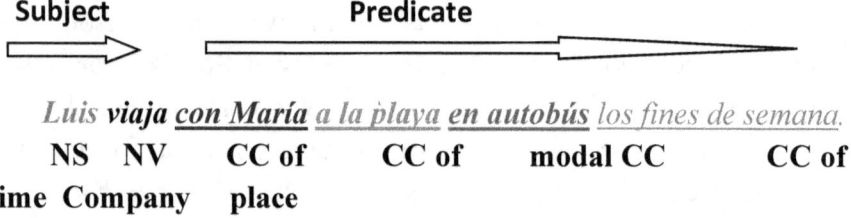

Luis **viaja** <u>**con María**</u> <u>*a la playa*</u> <u>**en autobús**</u> <u>los fines de semana</u>.
  NS   NV   CC of   CC of   modal CC   CC of time Company   place

Luis travels with Mary to the beach by bus on weekends

The interesting fact in Spanish, is that if you switch the positions of the CCs, the sentence won't lose its meaning and the structure will be grammatically correct. This gives the speaker or writer, the ability to "play" or be creative with the idea, without making any mistake.

Thus, there can be multiple results like these below:

- <u>Los fines de semana</u> <u>*a la playa*</u>

- <u>**En autobús**</u> *Luis* **viaja** <u>**con María**</u> <u>los fines de semana</u> <u>*a la playa*</u>

- *Luis* **viaja** <u>**con María**</u> <u>los fines de semana</u> <u>*a la playa*</u> <u>**en autobús**</u>

By learning and practicing, you can realize how "free" and "creative" Spanish can become as a language.

To complete this chapter, here are some exercises you can use as a practice

Exercise 1 In the next frame, try to replace the underlined words for: [lo], [los], [la], [las], [le], [les], according to the situation, if the complement is as direct or an indirect object.

Sentence (English)	Sentence (Spanish)	Replacement
He looks at the father's house.	Él mira **la casa del padre**.	Él **la** mira
You wash the baby's face.	Tú lavas la cara **al bebé**.	Tú **la** lavas
I pick up the papers from the floor.	Yo recojo **los papeles** del piso.	
Maria waters the plants.	María riega **las plantas**.	
The teacher teaches his students.	El profe enseña **a sus alumnos**.	
Juan brings candy for the girl.	Juan trae dulces **para la niña**.	
We buy food from the restaurant.	Compramos comida **al restaurante**.	
Daniel wants a phone.	Daniel quiere **un teléfono**.	

⚠️ Feelings in Spanish such as "like" or "love" work in a different form when using object pronouns:

- *"I love María"* is translated as "Yo amo **a** María" the preposition "a" is placed before the noun. And because there's a preposition, you might want to use an indirect pronoun to replace "María". But that would be an error in this specific situation. Check these two sentences as a translation for "I love her"

    Yo le amo ✖
    *Yo **la** amo* ✓

It's an exception but the logical meaning is that "love" in this case affects completely and directly the noun, even though you want to explain that you love "partially" it won't work with an IOP in

Chapter 6:

Sentences from a syntactic point of view

We already know that sentences are units of meaning and that they have grammatical coherence: they express meaning by themselves. You will have also noticed that in Spanish they begin with a capital letter and end with a period, and when it comes to interrogative or exclamatory sentences, their signs open and close them.

Precisely now, talking about grammatical coherence, in this chapter, you will learn about the different possibilities of how sentences can be structured in Spanish. As the title indicates, here we are addressing a part of the terrain of the syntax of the Spanish language, that is, the way in which word classes or categories are grouped and combined to generate grammatical sentences.

Based on what was discussed in previous chapters, here you are going to expand your knowledge on some concepts already developed, such as the notions of subject and predicate, also known as noun and verb phrases and the possibilities of their nuclei.

Content

- ➢ Predicative sentence
- ➢ Transitive and Intransitive sentence
- ➢ Attributive sentences

Part I: Predicative sentences

> The first part of this chapter If focused on predicative sentences. These are those that can be made up of a subject and a verbal predicate. **The nucleus of this predicate is any non-copulative verb** (other than the copulative verbs **ser, estar and parecer**).

For example: Daniel **plays** the guitar / Daniel always **thinks** about the guitar, these are predicative verbs because by themselves, they convey the idea of actions, which can be concrete or abstract.

On the contrary, copulative verbs by themselves are meaningless and in order for them to communicate something with explicit meaning, they must appear alongside other verbs (e.g. I **am happy** this morning).

Predicative verbs, unlike the previous ones, have full meaning (e.g. cry, eat, laugh…) Now, according to the verb type of the predicative sentences they are subdivided into transitive/ intransitive sentences.

But the possibilities of Spanish verbs can be not so fixed or permanent, always depending on the context. Regarding the above, the verb *to write* can be both transitive and intransitive depending on the context. Other verbs are always intransitive (e.g. *to die*) or always transitive (e.g. *to say*).

On the other hand, this type of verbs can be found in a sentence in active or passive form, as observed in the following examples:

- ➢ Active voice: Ezequiel **orders** food / "Ezequiel **ordena** comida"
- ➢ Passive voice: The room **was ordered** by Ezequiel / "La comida **fue ordenada** por Ezequiel

Transitive sentences.

They are those whose verb needs a direct complement, also known as a direct object (DO). These verbs need a complement and are therefore called transitive.

In these cases, the verb projects its action on the direct object or on a complement, which it modifies, alters or affects. For example:

Joaquin writes **songs** / "Joaquín escribe **canciones**"

Remember how you could check if it is a direct object or not: if we can replace it with <lo, los, la, las> it is, as in this example:

Joaquín writes **them**. / "Joaquín **las** escribe"

Another example:

We know **what you want to say** / "Sabemos **qué quieres decir**"
We know **it** / Nosotros **lo** sabemos"

Note in this example how in Spanish an DO needs to be mentioned with the transitive verbs. In other languages - English or Finnish, for example - explicit mention is not essential.

Intransitive Sentences

Intransitive sentences are those that do not have DO, can have indirect complement (IC / IO), or circumstantial complement (CC), but not DO.

Example:

> It rains every time I go out in the morning / **"Llueve cada vez que salgo en la mañana"**

Part II: Copulative or Attributive Sentences

> Copulative sentences, also known as attributive, are those that contain within them a nominal predicate (NP), which is formed by a copulative verb (***ser, estar. parecer***) and one or more attributes (modifiers of the subject).

So, the central function of the predicate is carried over to the attribute in question rather than the verb. For example: *The pool water is always very cool.*

Let us remember that in Spanish, as in other languages, there are a series of verbs that in some sentences lose their meaning and come to be used as copulative verbs complemented by an attribute. These verbs (also called semicopulatives) generate semi-attributive sentences, these are some of them:

- ➢ to result
- ➢ to continue
- ➢ to follow

- ➢ to resemble
- ➢ to lie
- ➢ to remain

Always remember to check the *"List of verbs"* provided in this book to enrich vocabulary.

Copulative or attributive sentences are completed with various complements: adjectives, nouns, pronouns, adverbs, infinitives or gerunds. Observe an example of each complement in the following table.

Complement	Attributive Sentence (English)	Attributive Sentence (Spanish)
Adjective	That picture is **wonderful.**	El cuadro es **maravilloso.**
Noun	The game is a **success.**	El juego es **una maravilla.**
Pronoun	The ball is **mine.**	El balón es **mío.**
Adverbs	Your plan is **better.**	Tu plan es **mejor.**
Infinitive form	The only thing left to do is **to paint.**	Lo único que le queda es **pintar.**
Gerund	I explain what he is **saying.**	Te explico lo que está **pintando.**

Chapter 7:

Adverbs

In a language, the adverb is the kind of word that, from the syntactic point of view, has the exclusive functions of modifying the adjective, another adverb and the verb directly only with circumstantial character. Let us remember that the noun, already explained, also has the ability to modify the verb but not only as circumstantial, like only the adverb can do.

Content

- ➢ Grammar of the adverb.
- ➢ Modifier function.
- ➢ Possibilities of being modified.
- ➢ Adverbial phrases.
- ➢ Morphology and semantics of the adverb.

Part I: Adverbs (Definition and Classification)

> In this chapter you will learn how adverbs work in Spanish, their place in a sentence, and how they are classified

Adverbs in Spanish don't work highly different from English. They can be placed after the verb and their function is the same. Modify or explain certain aspects of an action.

For example, quick, slow, a lot, a few, hard, well, bad, tomorrow, today, all those are or can be adverbs in Spanish when they are preceded by a verb. Check these examples:

"*The car goes fast*" / **"El carro va rápido"**

"*He does the work well* / *"El hace el trabajo bien"***

"*The turtle walks very slow* / **"La tortuga camina muy lento"**

They are describing the way the nouns apply or execute the action. When this happens, these words are called "adverbs".

➢ **Classification:**

Adverbs are classified into two large groups by their significance. The two (2) tables that appear on the following pages provide more details:

a) Adverbs of fixed significance:

b) Adverbs of occasional significance:

a) Adverbs of fixed significance:

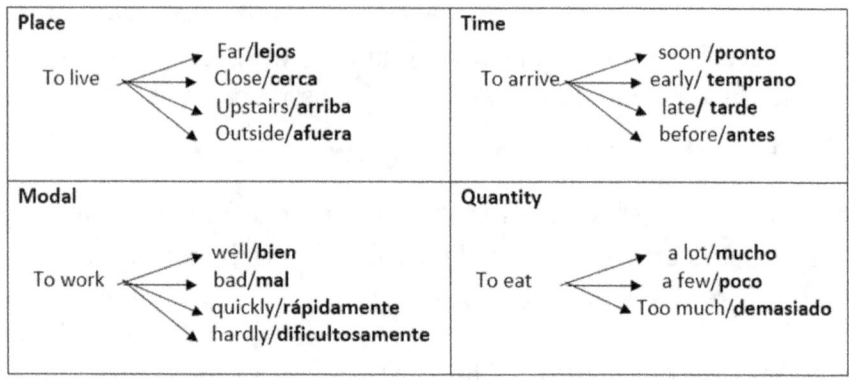

Also, words to deny or affirm an idea, to express "doubt" are also adverbs:

No / "No"
Never / "**Nunca**"
Neither / "**Tampoco**"
Yes / "**Sí**"
Surely / "**Seguramente**"
Maybe/ "**Quizás**"

⚠️ With the negative adverbs *"never", "neither", "no"*... In Spanish, **a negative sentence** in which one of these adverbs is present, the sentence must have two negative adverbs, in other words, **it has to be denied twice**. Check these examples:

- *I know no one* / **No conozco a nadie**
- *I don't want this either* / **Yo no quiero esto tampoco**
- *He doesn't come ever* / **Él no viene nunca**

Although, a sentence can only have one "negative" adverb and not require te use of "no". But in that case the structure is different.

- No one never comes here / **Nadie viene nunca aquí**
- Neither do you / **Tampoco tú**
- Never say never / **Nunca digas nunca**

b) Adverbs of occasional meaning :

Place	Time
Here/ "**aquí**"	Now / "**ahora**"
There / "**ahí**"	Today / "**hoy**"
Over there / "**allá**"	Yesterday / "**ayer**"
	Tomorrow / "**mañana**"
Modal	
Like that / "**así**"	

Part II: Variation

> Most of the adverbs are invariable. They have no accidents. There are some exceptions that the language community (usage) has imposed or normalized. So certain adverbs support diminutives and superlative degrees.

These variations are called accidents, and they have a diminutive or superlative degree to explain that the action it's be done in a higher or lower intensity:

> **Diminutive degree:** in this situation, an adverb can have suffixes like "-ito" or "-ico" to explain that either the action is done in a lower intensity. Check these examples:
>
>> *She eats **very little** amount of healthy food* / "Ella come **poquita** comida saludable"
>>
>> *I speak just **a little bit** of Spanish* / "Yo hablo **un poquito** de Español"
>>
>> *He does the homework a bit slow* / "Él hace la tarea **lentico**"

Superlative degree: in this case, the suffixes "-ísimo" and sometimes "-ito" can explain a higher intensity of the action's way of execution.

> *She arrives **very early*** / "Ella llega **tempranísimo/tempranito**"
>
> *I work **(really) too much*** / "Yo trabajo **muchísimo**" - ito is not applied.

You walk very very slow / "Tu caminas **lentísimo**"

They arrive always very late / "Ellos siempre llegan **tardísimo**"

> 💡 Spanish is a beautifully creative language, learning these variations, practicing, speaking, listening and reading will open more and more doors and break down many walls in order to let you be creative and understand the multiple ways Spanish words can be modified to explain additional qualities about them!

Chapter 8:

Creativity of the Spanish language

Within what is the effectiveness in linguistic communication, in natives and foreigners, lexical training is needed in favor of enrichment and conscious use of vocabulary. The opposite is destined for language poorness when speaking or writing, as instrumental manifestations of language. But the problem does not just stop there. Given the overlapping between production and linguistic reception, the speaker / writer in reference, lacking in vocabulary, will also feel limitations to understand as a listener or as a reader.

But to overcome stumbling blocks such as these, this manual has gathered tons of concepts to understand the most common vocabulary. And this chapter will offer you a practice guide for you to boost the comprehension of different words. Always remember: learning words from any language requires visual fixation, phonemic hearing, motor memory of the hand and familiarization through live use.

Content

> ➢ Derivation of the Spanish vocabulary

Part I: Derivation

> Derivation is a procedure in which a repertoire of words is formed from other existing words. We can say that they are terms linked to previous ones, keeping their lexical root. Precisely, this is the case thanks to two distinctive facts of the derivative lexicography: prefixing and suffixing, responsible for structuring word families.

The derivation not only enriches the vocabulary but also increases the possibility of satisfying the communication needs of its users.

- ➢ **Prefixation:** this is a lexical mechanism through which a word at its base (root or lexeme) undergoes changes of meaning by putting a particle called **a prefix** before it. For example:
    - o **To deny or express absence**: *in, des, a, contra*
    - o **Pro an idea:** *pro, para*
    - o **Matter:** *hemo* (blood), *hidro (wáter), electro (electricity)*
    - o **Size:** *híper, súper (big), mini (small)*
    - o **Quantity:** *mono* (one), *bi* (two);

Here some examples:

Inexplicable/**in**explicable
Counterforce/**Contra**fuerza
Abnormal/**A**normal
Pro-independentist/**Pro**independentista
Hydrotherapy/**Hidro**terapia
Supermarket/**Super**mercado
Bicycle/**Bi**cicleta

- **Suffixation:** this is a lexical mechanism through which a word at its base (root or lexeme) suffers nuances in its meaning by postponing a particle called suffix.

  For example:
  - *Quality:* ivo/iva
  - *Condition of:* dad
  - *Belief, movement:* ismo/ista
  - *Diminutive:* ito/ita
  - *Aumentative:* ote/ota

  Check this list with some examples:

  Caritative/caritat**ivo**,
  Creative/creat**ivo**
  Stability/estabili**dad**
  Racism,racist/rac**ismo**, rac**ista**
  Little girl/niñ**ita**
  Little house/cas**ita**
  Big house/cas**ota**
  Big kiss/bes**ote**

- **La derivación nominal:** this is the procedure of the language that allows to form nouns from other lexical categories. The base word can be a verb, a noun or an adjective. Check the following scheme:

In Spanish:

Verb to Noun		Noun to Noun		Adjective to Noun	
Cantar	canto	caza	cazador	bello	Belleza
Bailar	baile	gobernación	gobierno	bueno	Bondad
Regar	regadera	Libro	librería	amable	amabilidad
Volver	vuelta	Mesa	mesón	malo	Maldad
Caminar	caminata	Patín	patineta	leal	Lealtad

Jurar	juramento	Hierro	herrero	nuevo	novedoso
Confesar	confesión	mordida	mordedura	justo	Justicia
Saltar	salto	negocio	negociación	curioso	curiosidad
Elaborar	elaboración	Grito	gritadera	inteligente	inteligencia
Recibir	recibo	Gozo	gozadera	honrado	Honra
Aparecer	aparición	tobillo	tobillera	sabio	sabiduría
Sustituir	sustitución	edificio	edificación	honesto	honestidad
Elegir	elección	pintura	pintor	hermoso	hermosura
Reír	risa	Lápiz	lapicero	útil	Utilidad

In english:

Verb to Noun		Noun to Noun		Adjective to Noun	
Sing	Singing	Hunt	Hunter	Beautiful	Beauty
Dance	Dance	Governance	Government	Well	Goodness
Water	Shower	Book	Library	Kind	Kindness
Back	Lap	table	Big table	Bad (boy)	The evilness
Walk	Walk	Skate	Skateboard	Loyal	Loyalty
Swear	Oath	Iron	Blacksmith	New	innovative
Confess	Confession	Bite	The Bite	Just	Justice
Jump	Jump	Business	Negotiation	Curious	Curiosity
Develop	Development	Cry	screaming	Intelligent	Intelligence
Receive	Receipt	Joy	enjoyable	Honored	Honor
Appear	Appearance	Ankle	Anklet	Wise	Wisdom
Replace	Replacement	Building	edification	Honest	Honesty
Choose	Choice	Painting	Painter	Beautiful	Beauty
Laugh	Laughter	Pencil	Pen	Useful	Utility

This means that you can find a word and create or find derivations from its roots or "lexemes". Check this example with the root/lexeme **"mar"**/sea

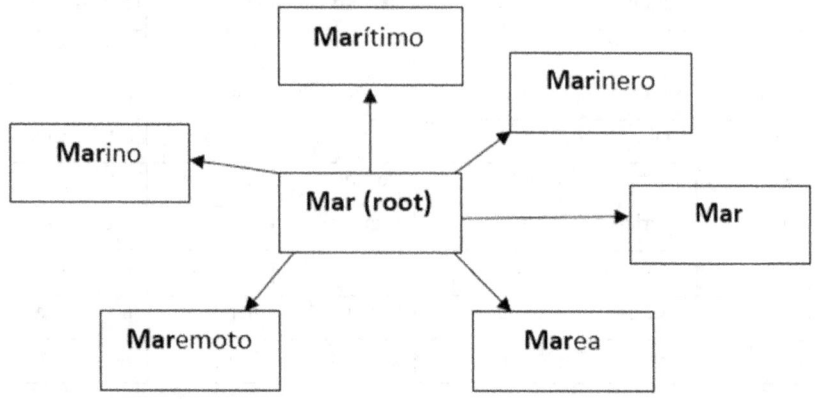

The root can create new words, all related to "the sea": *maritime, sailor, the sea, the tide, seaquake, marine*. In Spanish, this can be done with almost -because there are always exceptions- every word. Try to read, listen or speak with some native friends to find new words and the way they can be modified by adding prefixes or suffixes.

> **Sufijos apreciativos del español:** Given the cultural and idiosyncratic peculiarity of most Spanish-speaking countries, we include this section to highlight it and to familiarize yourself with the uses and valuations of some suffixes.

Compare, because in Spanish it is not the same saying:

- La camisa tiene una mancha. vs. - La camisa tiene un manchón.

In this example, *"The shirt has a stain"* vs. *"The shirt has a big stain"*

- Carlos vive en una casa. vs. - Carlos vive en un caserón.

In this example, *"Carlos lives in a house"* vs. *"Carlos lives in a huge house"*

- Esa chica es fea. vs. - Esa chica es feucha.

In this last example, *"That girl is ugly" vs. "that girl is a slightly ugly"*

These variations are due to specific evaluations given by speakers with a suffix to a word within the communicative context in question. Consequently, appreciative suffixes show subjectivities because they have a communicative emphasis, an affective charge directed at people, animals or things. In this sense, three (3) types can be established: diminutive (although it is not something small), augmentative (although it is not something big) and derogatory. Look at the following examples:

Este es mi niño pequeñito / *This is my little boy.* (Positive affection).

Juan está grandote / *Juan is so big.* (Positive affection).

Vive en una casa feísima / *She lives in a very ugly house.* (Irony or dislike).

¿Te vas con esa mujercita? / Do you go out with that little woman? (Irony or comptent).

From this amazing last chapter, you can absorb very important facts:

- The variation or creativity in Spanish is outstanding
- Suffixes or prefixes can be used to change the intensity or add a positive or negative meaning
- You can boost your vocabulary by understanding how the word is composed and trying to change their morphemes

This is a language you can enjoy practicing because of its multiple possibilities to modify sentences, nouns, adjectives, adverbs and many other words!

Vocabulary

We want to complete the content of this book by offering a useful list of daily-life vocabulary. Here, you can find verbs and their conjugations and some words related to specific topics like "food", "sports", "travelling" …

Content

- ➢ Verbs and vocabulary related to different topics:
  - o Travelling
  - o Daily routine
  - o Food
  - o Home
  - o At the restaurant
  - o To give an opinion
  - o Visiting places
  - o Socializing

With this vocabulary, this book wants to gather all the information given before and add new useful words for daily life.

The content is divided into topics. Each topic has vocabulary and verb lists.

➢ Travelling

Activity	Translation	Nouns	Translation
To arrive	Llegar	Beach	Playa
To book	Reservar	Bus	Autobús
To buy	Comprar	City	Ciudad
To call	Llamar	Country	País
To call	Llamar	Hotel	Hotel
To come	Venir	Lake	Lago
To go	Ir	Map	Mapa
To know	Saber	Money	Dinero
To pay	Pagar	Mountain	Montaña
To reserve	Reservar	Plane	Avión
To search	Buscar	Room	Habitación
To sleep	Dormir	Ship	Embarcacion
To travel	Viajar	State	Estado
To visit	Visitar	Taxi	Taxi
To wait	Esperar	Ticket	Boleto
To walk	Caminar	Town	Pueblo

➢ Daily Routine

Activity	Translation	Nouns	Translation
To do exercise/To workout	Hacer ejercicio	Bed	Cama
To get dressed	Vestirse	Breakfast	Desayuno
To drive	Manejar/Conducir	Car	Coche
To get back home	Regresar a casa	Dinner	Cena
To go to sleep	Ir a dormir	House/home	Casa Hogar
To go to the bathroom	Ir al baño	Internet	Internet
To have breakfast	Desayunar	Lunch	Almuerzo
To have dinner	A cenar	News	Noticias
To have lunch	Almorzar	Newspaper	Periódico
To take a nap	Tomar una siesta	Shower	Ducha
To take a shower	Tomar una ducha	Television	Televisión
To wake up/To get up	Despertarse / levantarse	Work	Trabajo

➢ Food

Activity	Translation	Nouns	Translation
To add	Agregar	Cheese	Queso
To boil	Hervir	Fish	Pescado
To cook	Cocinar	Jam	Jamón
To cut	Cortar	Meat	Carne
To drink	Beber	Food	Comida
To serve	Servir	Dish	Plato
To eat	Comer	Vegetales	Vegetales
To freeze	Congelar	Bread	Un pan
To fry	Freir	Potato	Patata
To measure	Para medir	Onion	Cebolla
To prepare	Preparar	Chicken	Pollo
To slice	Cortar en rodajas	Butter	Mantequilla

➢ Home

Activity	Translation	Nouns	Translation
To arrange	Vivir	Bathroom	Baño
To clean	Trapear	Bedroom	Dormitorio
To live	Arreglar	Home/house	Inicio / casa
To mop	Mudarse	Kitchen	Cocina
To move	Limpiar	Living room	Sala
To paint	Quedarse	Sofa	Sofá
To stay	Lavar	The basement	El sótano
To sweep	Barrer	The ceiling	El techo
To wash	Pintar	Yard	Patio

➢ At the restaurant

Activity	Translation	Nouns	Translation
To drink	Beber	Bad	Malo
To eat	Comer	Chef	Chef
To enjoy	Disfrutar	cutlery	cuchillería
To order	Ordenar	Food	Comida
To pay	Pagar	fork	tenedor
To take away	Para llevar	glass	vaso
To try	Probar	Good	Bueno
To visit	Visitar	Knife	Cuchillo
		Menu	Menú
		Spoon	Cuchara
		Waiter(tress)	Mesero(a)

➢ To give an opinion

Activity	Translation	Nouns	Translation
To agree	Llegar a un acuerdo	Argument	Argumento
To argue	Argumentar	Belief	Creencia
To believe	Creer	dicussion	discusión
To discuss	Para discutir	Idea	Idea
To give an opinion	Dar una opinión	Mind	Mente
To learn	Aprender	Opinion	Opinión
To share	Para compartir	Plan	Plan
To solve	Resolver	Strategy	Estrategia
To talk	Hablar	The terms	Los términos
To think	Pensar	Thinking	Pensando

➢ Visiting places (mountain, beach, lake)

Activity	Translation	Nouns	Translation
To bathe	Bañarse	Beach	Playa
To breath	Respirar	clouds	Nubes
To dive	Bucear	Lake	Lago
To camp	Acampar	Mountain	Montaña
To rest	Descansar	Nature	Naturaleza
To swim	Nadar	Sand	Arena
To tan	Broncearse	Sky	Cielo
To visit	Visitar	Sun	Sol
To walk	Caminar	Water	Agua

➢ Socializing

Activity	Translation	Nouns	Translation
To dance	Bailar	A call	Una llamada
To greet	Saludar	Dancing	Baile
To hang out	Salir	A Drink	Bebida
To have fun	Divertirse	Friend	Amigo(a)
To meet	Reunirse	Meeting	Reunión
To party	Hacer una fiesta	Movie theather	Cine
To say good-bye	Despedirse	Movies	Películas
To send a message	Enviar un mensaje	Music	Música
To text	Textear	Party	Fiesta

www.ingramcontent.com/pod-product-compliance
Lightning Source LLC
Chambersburg PA
CBHW071432070526
44578CB00001B/86